"I Wanna Tell You A Story!"

Max Bygraves

"I Wanna Tell You
A Story!"

MAX BYGRAVES

For Margaret
xx

Max Bygraves
1995

W. H. Allen · London

A Howard & Wyndham Company

Printed and bound in Great Britain by

Butler & Tanner Ltd,

Frome and London

for the Publishers, W. H. Allen & Co. Ltd

44 Hill Street, London W1X 8LB

ISBN 0 491 01596 8

DEDICATED TO
Old Lil Bygraves
with my thanks

Introduction

It's a fact that people in show business have to keep very late hours at night and sleep very long hours in the morning.

We have a saying that goes "Early to bed, early to rise—means you must be out of work."

So, one morning, there I was behaving in the traditional manner —eyes shut, mouth open and doing a fairly good vocal impression of a man sawing wood, when I was aroused by a loud knocking on the front door. I shook my wife: "Someone," I said, "is knocking on the front door."

She opened one eye and murmured: "Well, it isn't me—is it?" And promptly went back to sleep.

The knocking continued, so, making a mental note to get a divorce, give up show business and do away with the front door, I went below to plead with the door knocker to stop.

I also noticed it was 7.30 in the morning. I'd forgotten they had a 7.30 in the morning—I knew they had a 7.30 in the evening—it usually comes before they call "Curtain Up!"

Dragging myself to the door, I opened it and there in all his morning glory was the postman.

"Mister Bygraves?"

I didn't answer for a moment, I was thinking, "Why is it that only dogs are allowed to bite postmen?"

"Yes."

"I've got a letter for you, sir."

I said, "Look friend, don't think I'm trying to teach you your job but the other postmen have got rather a novel way of delivering a letter—they push them through this flap here—the letter box."

His friendly manner vanished. "I have a letter here, sir, on which the postage has not been paid—if you wish me to hand you the letter, you must pay the sum of 17 pence." He waved the envelope, "Take it—or leave it."

"Who's it from?" I asked.

"I don't write 'em, sir, I only deliver 'em."

7

He was beginning to enjoy this and I was beginning to regret that remark about the letter box.

"Would you mind waiting a moment please, postman?"

"Don't be long, sir—we do not have all day." His enunciation was beginning to worry me.

The only money I could find was a five pound note. I shook my wife gently. "Darling—have you got any small change?" With her eyes still shut, she instinctively grabbed the fiver and said, "No, I haven't." And went back to sleep. Already it was an expensive letter.

I tiptoed into my youngest daughter's room; it seemed a shame to wake her from that childish slumber. I shook her gently and whispered: "Darling—where's your small change?"

She smiled drowsily, "You *must* be joking!" And straight back to Dreamland she went.

Meanwhile, back at the door: "I haven't got all day, sir!"

"Look, postman," I pleaded, "I haven't got 17 pence but I must have that letter."

The milkman was coming up the drive; an idea!

"Milkman, could you possibly lend me 17p?"

The milkie looked at me, then at my Rolls Royce parked in the drive and with a knowing look to the postman, he produced 17 pence, said a silent goodbye to the "ready" and handed it to me without a word.

I paid for the letter and watched the two of them walk away in low, ominous conversation.

I tore the letter open—it was from the publishers and it began ". . . Dear Sir, we would be delighted to publish any ideas you might have on humour, the world is short of laughter, especially in print, etc., etc."

The only reason I am writing this book is in the hope that it will sell at least four copies and I will get a royalty of three and a half pence per book, that way I hope to get part of my investment back and also our milkman's friendship.

MAX BYGRAVES

8

PART 1

"BACK IN MY CHILDHOOD DAYS"

WORDS AND MUSIC BY MAX BYGRAVES

The things that we did
When I was a kid
Keep coming back to me

The games that we played
The friends that we made
Keep haunting my memory.

I get so nostalgic
Remembering when
The biff bat and the yo-yo were the craze

Garbo and Myrna Loy
Ambrose and Harry Roy
They were my childhood days.

© LANTERN MUSIC LTD

On the afternoon of 16 October 1922, a young boxer named Battling Tom Smith of Bermondsey was fighting an eight-round contest at The Ring, Blackfriars, London. He lost on points and received thirty shillings. With his gloves, shoes, etc., in a brown paper bag, he ran for a 68 tram that took him to Rotherhithe a few miles away. There, in his two-room council flat, he peered through puffed eyes at his second son, born a few hours earlier. He checked that the new-born infant had no deformities, made sure his fists were in good shape, left the thirty shillings he had earned with his wife and dashed for a bus to take him to Stepney, where he fought the same evening a ten-round contest. He won and received £10.

So, on the day I was born, my parents were rich, having something like £12 in the "pot". I have been told with that money my father bought a suit, fixed up my mother with a new coat and hat, bought the groceries for the week, paid two weeks' rent (having been behind one week) and still had £6 left.

The flat was a rabbit hutch that comprised a living room, a bedroom, a loo and a domestic quarter—in this section, which measured ten feet by four feet, was a gas stove, a copper, a sink with a cold water tap and shelves holding various saucepans; there was a gas jet with a fish-tail flame coming from it and because of the copper being in constant use, the walls were for ever covered with condensation.

There was a passage from the front room to the street door; why it was called the "street door" I've never worked out because we were on the first floor, overlooking a square that had iron posts about five feet tall with pulleys attached—these were used to loop lines through to hang washing on.

At either end of the square were five large dustbins that looked like gigantic oil drums—the flat dwellers took their garbage, it was mostly ashes from their coal fires and tea leaves, there for collection. If we ever saw a Libby's or John West salmon tin amongst this rubbish, we knew somebody had had a winning bet with the bookie on the corner, or done a successful mugging.

There were twenty families to a block of flats and there were eleven blocks in all. In the early twenties they were occupied by mostly young newly-weds like my parents but these newly-weds were breeding like rabbits, so by the time I was around ten years of age, the place seemed to be running alive with kids—and mice and bugs. My parents had fought a losing battle trying to rid us of these vermin. As soon as they fumigated, they went next door. When the next door neighbours did the same, they came back to us.

The "buildings" were only twenty yards from the River Thames. Alongside the river were the wharves; these wharves had rats as big as elephants and they would come down after dark to our dustbins and eat our garbage. The favourite game was to stalk them with half a house brick and try to knock them senseless. I can remember stalking several but can't recall ever "exterminating" any.

Most of the men worked in the Surrey Commercial Docks. Some were lucky and had regular jobs but most, my father was one, were casual labourers. When there were plenty of boats to be unloaded, there was enough work for all; when there were only a few, less men were needed. If you looked big and strong, you were "called on" by the gang boss, known as the "ganger". My father was a flyweight and not very tall, although very strong for his size. He was often not seen by the ganger so he would traipse back to the employment exchange with hundreds of others and "sign on". He was still boxing but was getting past his prime—there were a lot more youngsters willing to be punched about for that quick purse of three or four pounds. Slowly he had to give up fighting in the ring and became a "full time unemployed casual dock labourer".

From the time my memory starts working for me—I was eight or nine—my mother had had two more children, both girls, Lily and Patricia. She had moved into the living-room with my father and they shared the only double bed we had. We four kids slept in the bedroom. My brother Harry, eighteen months my senior, and I shared a single bed; Lil and Pat shared another single brass bedstead with quite a lot of rampant bed bugs.

I can remember my first day at school—I was five—the teacher gave us all a slate and we had to go and mend the roof.

The school was in Paradise Street. The joker who gave the street that name had a great sense of humour. This street had almost everything in it: a sawmill, an iron foundry, another block of flats similar to ours, a fire station, a grocer's, five pubs, a Catholic church, and a police station. On Sunday mornings, the men from the Irish families, and there were dozens of them, would go to eleven o'clock mass, come out and go into one of the pubs, an hour or two later they would have a glorious punch up and be behind bars; all this before two o'clock. What's more, they didn't have to travel more than thirty yards to get blessed, get drunk, get arrested and get fined.

I had a good sense of rhythm as a kid: being baptised a Catholic, it would be a great asset. I learned most of my songs from a gramophone with a big horn. Most of the records were by bands. We bought them in Petticoat Lane for a penny each and the labels had names like "Winner", "Eclipse", "Regal Zonophone"—the one I remember most vividly was Leslie Sarony singing "Rhymes" because we put our own "dirty" words to this. I can recall getting a stinging smack on the ear from my father who heard me giving out with:

> There was a young man from Newcastle
> Who picked up a brown paper parcel
> On it was writ and in it was ——
> A present from Old Gandhi's ——.

The crudeness of these songs would shock the grown-ups, yet it was quite common for them to "eff and blind".

Once at school, I was sent for in the classroom to go down to the infants and take my sister home as she had "messed" her drawers. I had never heard it put that way—"messed" was real upper class. I didn't take her home, I took her to the shore of the river. I must have been about eight and she was six. I got her to step out of her "drawers", telling her to put her frock over her head, I "dunked" her in the water till she came out clean. When she had washed her knickers out, she put them back on. A gentleman had watched us do all this from a wharf and as we ascended the stairs to go and play for the rest of the day, he shouted, "You dirty little sod!" Goodness knows what he thought I'd been up to.

There were street cries from the vendors who made a living going from door to door. One of these was "Scrag", the cats' meat man. Scrag had a big wicker basket filled with pink-looking horse meat that he put on a wooden skewer. He did this walking along and between calls he'd pop a bit of the meat into his mouth. Most flats had cats for several reasons: one was to keep the mice away; another was to kick when things went wrong; and a third was as a waste disposal for fish bones and scraps—if you could give the cat a morsel that made it lick the plate, it also saved washing up.

Scrag would enter the "buildings" ejecting a sound like a klaxon horn, he was actually saying "Meat" but the way he did it through his nose it came out "Mate". As he entered our manor he'd have several cats, who knew the time he arrived, following him. He'd give a loud rat-tat on the doors, hand the skewered meat in, collect a penny and go on his way.

Sometimes he'd have a dozen or more kids, me included, in his wake, all impersonating his cry of "Mate". When Scrag got fed up with this, he had a genteel way of dismissing us by spinning round and saying: "Piss off, or I'll put my toe up your arses!"

We would all then run off chanting: "Walla—walla—cats' meat— eat brown bread—Ever see a sausage fall down dead?"

Another town crier was "Skates"—he sold fish from a two-wheeled barrow with a flat wooden top covered with fresh fish, mostly herring, haddock and cod. It was good fish—I don't think hundreds of flies could be wrong *every* time he came.

"Skatesy", as he was referred to, had a cry that went: "Gityer-bloater!" This, translated, meant "Get your bloaters!" As he shouted this cry, thick veins would stand out on his neck. So forceful was the cry, he only did it twice, once as he entered the buildings and once more about five minutes after. If my mother could afford it and my father had landed a day's work, I was sent to Mr Skates for a piece of haddock. I was always told to ask for "middle only". This annoyed him tremendously, he often muttered: "You can't all have bloody middles—somebody's got to have the tails." He tried to get over this by letting a customer have a middle cut one week and a tail cut the following week. He was pretty useless at remembering and if he tried to bung us a tail piece, we would tell him we had tail the week before. We hadn't, but he could never remember our faces.

I would take the haddock home, my mother would boil it, time it to the second, then, as my dad walked through the door, she would have it ready on the table, steaming with a blob of margarine on. We kids would stand and watch him devour it with several thick slices of bread and margarine, plus two or three cups of tea.

Sometimes, as a tit-bit, he'd pop a piece into our mouths and it tasted better than anything I have ever tasted in my life—and that includes caviar and smoked salmon, two dishes that I adore now that I can afford them.

One day, Skatesy didn't come round. We heard that he was ill with a throat infection. Without his cry of "Gityerbloater!" people couldn't tell the time any more. He was so precise each day that you could time your clocks by him. He died and nobody ever replaced him.

"The Indian toffee man" was another caller. He was an Indian with an off-white turban round his head, who walked through the streets with a little tinkling bell—he had no voice, just this little bell that he tinkled gently. It could be heard from great distances. For a ha'penny he would lift the lid of a tin box that was strapped round his shoulder in the same way usherettes carry ice-cream trays. Inside he had pieces of newspaper about six inches square, these he would roll into a small cone and fill with a whiskery sort of toffee, rather like candy floss. It came in various colours: pink being the most popular.

The Indian was a tall, thin, gangling man with a permanent smile. He always wore soft shoes and seemed to glide along. We called him Mick.

One hot summer day, we came across him fast asleep in a doorway. He had taken his tin off and it was a good yard away from him. He didn't wake up as we got near so, on tip-toe, we took the box round the corner and helped ourselves to this toffee that we all adored. As I was stuffing a handful of it into a piece of newspaper I had taken from inside the box, I looked up to see him coming towards me, the smile was gone and the eyes were flashing and he was cursing in his own language.

I slammed the lid down and ran, he chased me for fifty yards or so. I was frightened because we believed in those days that all murders were done by Indians who carved people up with those curved knives. He obviously thought that his box was more important, however, and gave up the chase. I kept running for another hour to make sure I had shaken him off.

After that day, whenever I heard the tinkle of his bell, I would hide myself in our coal cupboard until I thought he had gone, convinced that if he ever saw me again I'd be cut up in little pieces and sold to the cats' meat man.

King George wore a monocle
We read the *News Chronicle*
Back in my childhood days.

There was Gandhi and Lenin
Lady Astor and Bevin
Back in my childhood days.

We all use t' cram
On a sixty-eight tram
The railways didn't have those long delays.

And to go thro' your hair
Nitty Nora was there
Back in my childhood days.

Nitty Nora was the woman I dreaded most—this was a woman sent from the Council to go through our heads for lice and fleas. After she had been through our hair with a fine tooth-comb, we were marked to go to the clinic for delousing. The following morning we were collected by coach and taken to Spa Road where, with dozens of other kids, our heads were washed in soft soap and then rubbed with Lysol. To make us feel more embarrassed the other kids who saw us get out of the coach would run rings around us shouting "Unclean! Unclean!"

My father's way of keeping our heads clean was to invest two shillings in a pair of clippers. My brother and I had to have the lot off about every three weeks. The clippers would pull and we'd have great ridges where he had "gone against the grain". To hide our embarrassment, we wore cloth caps, but the other kids knew that beneath was a newly shorn head, they crept up behind, knocked our caps off and smacked us on the nut with a wet hand, shouting "check", as it made a loud slapping noise.

Harry and I had so many fights trying to stop this we got the name of the "fighting Bys"—the By was short for Bygraves and was later changed to "Pie". I was known as Wally Pie and it stuck right till the day I left home, ten years later. Harry is still called Harry Pie to this day.

Most of us kids were thieves. All of us stole in one way or another. I have stayed in touch with quite a few of my school friends and of the half dozen boys I played with, at least four of them have been guests of HM Prisons—a couple of them for quite long stretches.

The shop that came easiest for "nicking" was Mrs Marlow's, just outside the buildings. (The shop is there to this very day and is almost the same as it looked all those years ago.) She was a big fat lady who dressed in black. She kept her money in a string bag underneath her black apron. She had a greengrocery shop that also sold coal. The goods were laid out round the shop and our

21

favourite trick was to ask for a penny Oxo cube. These she kept in a tin in the back room because by law she shouldn't have sold them. As soon as she waddled off to get them, we did a quick "nick"—we'd take apples, oranges, even cauliflowers, and toss them to an accomplice outside the shop who would have to be a good catcher then, as she reappeared, he would disappear. I would be wearing an angelic smile with the penny for the Oxo cube at the ready, then we'd go behind a wharf door and eat the spoils.

Once I made a big mistake. I gave Mrs Marlow the money for the beef cube and watched her waddle off to the back room. I decided on that day I was going to help myself to a large Jaffa orange. These were neatly stacked in a pyramid in the window. I wasn't tall enough to reach the top one so reached out and took one from the bottom, the whole pyramid came tumbling down and I stood there knee deep in large Jaffa oranges. She came back into the shop, stopped, looked at me, looked at the oranges all over the place and said: "Who did that?" I shook my head. "They fell!" I said. I helped her pick them all up again—all the time I felt her eyeing me, asking herself whether they had fallen by themselves or whether I had caused it by helping myself to one. When we finished picking them up, she gave me an apple for helping her. After Mrs Marlow's we moved on to bigger things.

Almost every boy had his own soap-box cart. This was a soap-box on old pram wheels that we made ourselves; this made us mobile thieves. I can remember going to a certain road that was fenced by boards about nine feet tall and eight inches wide. On the other side of the fence was the docks and when the dock workers finished at five o'clock, we would be standing there with our soap-box near a particular spot that had been selected. I didn't know exactly what was happening at first but it worked like this. My friend Billy had arranged with his father to wait at this particular spot, then his father would arrive on the other side of the fence, because he was liable to be searched at the gate, and he got rid of his loot by throwing it over the top of the fence to Billy. Over would come tins of peaches, corned-beef, pilchards, etc. Then my friend Billy would put them in the soap-box, cover them with a sack and I would then push him back to the buildings. Billy's dad would then walk through the gate "clean".

If my father had ever found out about this, he would have punished me by belting me—he had a thick leather belt that he used on me only three or four times, each time for dishonesty. He had a great code of honour and even had we been starving he would not have done anything criminal. He was really too honest for that area. If he found out about my misdemeanours, he'd make me get down on my knees and recite an Act of Contrition, this I found most embarrassing: I think I'd rather have been belted by him.

Oswald Mosley seems to be the political leader uppermost in my mind from those days. Once, I was warned by my parents not to go anywhere near Millpond Bridge on one particular Sunday when I was eight or nine. It was the day of a big Fascist rally. Of course, I went.

Everywhere were men in cloth caps, mounted policemen were patrolling the area; foot policemen with tunics that buttoned up to the neck were ready to link arms to hold the crowd back.

From a dairy shop doorway, Alfie Roberts, a boyhood friend and myself stood on two steel milk crates to watch the proceedings. A great deal of booing and hissing broke out as a big black car came into sight and from it stepped Oswald Mosley. He stepped up to a wooden sort of pulpit that had been erected. There was a large microphone in front of it that almost covered his face and, though I understood nothing of what was going on, I could continually hear the word "Jews" mentioned. The men around were fairly quiet listening to this oration, until suddenly a man a few yards in front of me tossed a cabbage towards the speaker and then fighting broke out everywhere.

The mounted policemen began to charge—they wielded long batons and were hitting out at any head that had a cap on. Men were falling and lying about in pools of blood. Alfie and I looked on wide-eyed; it was the first real violence I had ever witnessed.

A tough-looking stevedore, seeing us in the doorway, shouted, "Come on you two—this is no place for kids!" Had he left us where we were, we'd have been all right, but he decided to get us to safety. He lifted us down from the milk crates and decided to rush us across the road. As we reached halfway, I tripped in one of the tram lines that went along the middle of the road. Men were falling everywhere and suddenly the man who had decided to run us to a safe part, got a loud clump on the side of his head. He left me and staggered off like a drunk. I crouched there not knowing which way to run.

23

A mounted policeman yelled, "Give me your hand!" I gave him my hand and he yanked me up into the saddle exactly the same way as I had seen Hoot Gibson and Tom Mix do it at the flicks.

He seated me in front of him and we charged off down the road. When we were out of the scuffle, he dropped me on to the pavement and said, "Go on home!"

I ran all the way home. I got inside the flat and announced to everybody that I had just had a ride on a horse.

"Whose horse?" said my father.

"A policeman's horse."

"Where?"

"Up at Millpond Bridge."

"You were told not to go to Millpond Bridge," said my mother.

"I forgot," I lied.

"Well, this will help you remember," said my father as he gave me a clout round the ear.

There were no luxury holidays. When the schools broke up, we hung around the district or had a "day out". Most of these days were spent at Southwark Park—a large park with a junior and senior playground and some large fields where we played for the whole day. We would have a bottle or two of yellow lemonade that we made ourselves by putting lemon crystals in water and shaking it. For lunch we usually had several thick slices of bread and jam or, if things weren't so good, we'd just dip the bread in sugar.

If it was springtime, we'd wait for the park bell to ring—this would mean we had to vacate the park—then we would nip over the railings and lift a few tulip bulbs that had been put in to grow. We'd store them in the brown paper bag we had our lunch in, then walk past the "parkie", who would be waiting there to lock the gates. The bulbs we'd take home and put into two window boxes and as the blooms appeared there'd be great excitement. We always told our father we'd found them on waste ground and dug them up.

He nursed the shoots and would often send us out with a bucket and shovel to pick up horse dung as fertiliser. We thought nothing of walking into the flat with it while everybody was having tea. My father would take it, then pat it into the soil; he was always

24

reluctant to throw any away. We had some of the healthiest flowers around.

One old lady we called Granny Adams wore a cloth skivvy cap and would be forever cleaning the brass knocker outside her door. It was spotless. When her husband died, she suddenly "got delusions of grandeur". One of the stories going around about her was that she would go to the grocery shop, buy half a pound of coffee, sprinkle it on the three feet by four landing outside her flat, then write to relatives saying she had "just been for a walk in the grounds".

The days we looked forward to the most were the Holiday Mondays. This meant the fair would be at Blackheath, a tuppenny tram ride from Rotherhithe Tunnel, the fare stage we boarded at.

They were massive affairs. The coconut shies alone stretched for a quarter of a mile. Every stall was a magical wonder to us. There were dodgems, walls of death, big dippers, roll a penny, penny arcades. It was a wonderland.

When we knew it was coming up to a Bank Holiday, my brother and myself would go to a piece of waste ground and get a stick about eighteen inches long—on top of it, we would press some old newspaper into the shape of a coconut—then, we'd go back to the regulation line (it was halfway for children) and practise hitting the paper with an old cricket ball. We would practise for hours on end until we could knock the paper down ten out of ten times.

On the big day we would go to Blackheath with our couple of bob pocket money, then slowly walk up and down eyeing the shies —we were convinced that half the coconuts were glued in and unless we saw them falling fairly easy from the stands that held them, we'd give them a miss.

When we found a likely stall, we'd pay our threepence for seven balls and take up our positions. Once Harry and myself got eleven coconuts with fourteen balls, so accurate had we become.

On this day we debated whether to spend another threepence on another seven balls because we could sell a coconut for three-pence to almost any of the people in the fairground—it seemed a nice profit. We walked up to the barker to buy another seven balls but he said: "Piss off." We looked at him blankly and he quietly said again, eyeing our brown carrier bag which now contained twenty coconuts or more, "Piss off—you've got enough as it is."

My brother had the measure of this particular stall and he didn't want to leave it. He told me to walk over to a policeman and ask him the time. I did this, then asked him if he knew the route of the forty-seven bus. The barker could see me talking away to the bobby, who was only a few paces away. Harry then told him that I was talking to my father the policeman, and could he have another seven balls. The fellow practically gave them to Harry. He got another four coconuts—*then* we pissed off.

If we ever got sick
We were rubbed in with Vick
Back in my childhood days

Zam Buk and Germolene
Boracic and Thermogene
Back in my childhood days.

Friday was bath night
With Syrup of Figs
We'd spit it out all over the place.

A cake cost a farthing
So why were we starving?
Back in my childhood days.

Our main diet was stew. When my mother wasn't pregnant she worked for Fisher's Wharf sorting bad butter beans from good butter beans. She would pocket a pound or two of these, which were "perks", and bring them home. In another pocket she'd have pearl barley. With a few carrots and some onions she'd make a stew —we had this four or five times a week, sometimes with some scrag-end in it, sometimes without. If my father had happened to get a day's work, we'd have a rabbit and at Christmas we'd have a chicken—that was a real luxury. We never complained about the food but sometimes we'd go up on the roof and throw slates down.

When I was ten, I found out about girls—up till then I thought the forbidden fruit was prunes, and 38-21-36 was my mother's Co-op number.

I also found out that if you can make a girl laugh, you are pretty certain to "have it away". I had learned to do a pretty good impression of Sandy Powell from some of his recordings and I could sing a fair song. I also found out that if the conditions are right, there's nothing an adult likes to hear more than a kid sing grown-up words. For instance, I used to sing "Melancholy Baby"—I didn't know what melancholy meant—neither did half of the grown-ups but it was good musically. From these songs I went on to sing at parties. The grown-ups would have a "whip round" and give me a hat full of coppers. It was better than thieving.

So with my impressions and my rendering of "Melancholy Baby" I was making some nice pocket money. The only trouble was, I kept seeing the same faces at the same parties and in time I became a "has been". To be a "has been" at ten is not a pleasant thought; I had to get a larger repertoire.

We were still living in the same two rooms but the family was larger, we had two more sisters and my grandfather had moved in —this made nine in all: my mother and father, my brother and me, four sisters and grandad, if one of us got out of bed to go to the "loo" during the night, we had to leave a book-mark in our place.

The Depression had got worse. There was less money and there were more mouths to feed. It was expected that we should help financially, although we were still at school. My brother had a milk round in the morning and I had a paper round at night. With a quire of papers, *Star*, *News* and *Standard* under my arm, I'd deliver to the people who mostly bought them to look through the small ads, job hunting.

A quire of papers is quite a load for a boy to hump up ten flights of stairs, so what I did was to leave what I didn't need on the ground floor and run the rest up the stairs. I soon packed this up when I noticed on one particular block, I finished a couple of papers short when I cashed in. Some old codger would come out of his flat as soon as he heard me mount the stairs and nick a couple of them. I told my father that this was happening so he told me to do as I usually did and he would watch to see if this was so.

Sure enough when I had gone upstairs, the man came out and helped himself to a *News* and *Standard*—my father saw him do it, he then went over, knocked at the door and said: "You bloody old thief." The old codger took a swing at my father, whose natural instinct was to duck and counterpunch—the neighbour finished up with his jaw in a plaster cast for the next three months. Every time I got to his flat from then on I would tip-toe past and deliver my papers.

We lived as a tribe; if we knew a neighbour was living on his wits we never discussed it. When the "tecs" in their plainclothes came snooping, putting out feelers, we were always wide-eyed and knew nothing.

There was a voter named Bugeye Smith who stole the safe from the local railway station. To hide the noise of sawing to get it open, they played the piano and sang all night, but when the law came to ask questions, we all said we heard nothing. He was caught and sent to prison for eighteen months. On the day he was sentenced, I can remember a couple of ladies coming round for a collection towards the upkeep of his wife and kids—what's more, everybody at every flat donated something.

When a family is poor and there are a lot of them, they seem to need footwear more than anything else—this was costing my parents every bit of spare cash they had. At twelve I had started going to evening classes, this was voluntary. We could do woodwork, metal-work, shoe-repairing and gymnasium. I got very interested in shoe-repairing and would take five or six pairs a week to repair. I became quite an expert and could make a job almost as good as any "snob" who charged four times as much as I could do them for. By doing the family footwear, I was saving my parents quite a lot.

Because of the classes closing for summer holidays, I decided to go in business for myself—I bought a couple of lasts, one for men's, one for ladies' shoes, hammers, nails and heel ball. The only work-shop available to me was the "loo", which wasn't much bigger than a telephone booth. I would sit most evenings for several hours mending the neighbours' and family footwear. Of course, I had a lot of interruptions as my seat was the actual WC with a board across the top. If there was a knock on the door by somebody who couldn't wait, I had to put all my gear to one side, lift the board and go outside, sometimes they'd be in and out in a couple of minutes, other times I'd have to wait another fifteen minutes to let the air clear.

Max (*the tallest*), brother Harry on his left, father, mother, Lil,
Pat and Kathleen.

MAX BYGRAVES

Top left: an act with Roger Welch (*Vera Lynn's brother*).

Bottom left: winner of RAF talent contest, 1943.

Above: Max with manager Jock Jacobsen (1948).

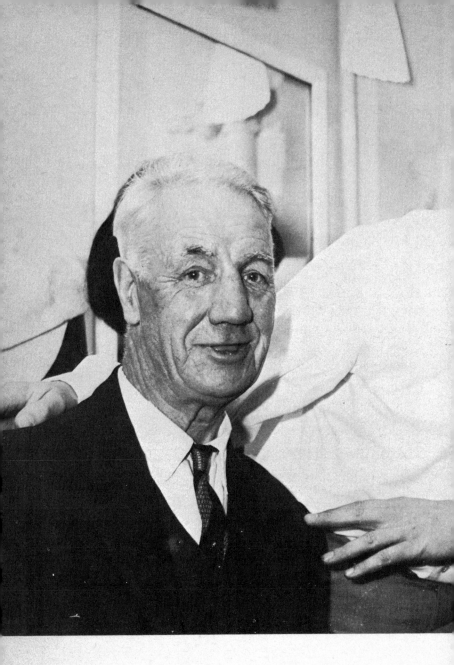

Max with mother and father.
Inset: the Hippodrome before its conversion
to the Talk of the Town (1956).

VAL PARNELL PRESENTS

MAX
BYGRAVES
IN A NEW
FUN SONG & DANCE SHOW
meet me on
the corner
6.15 TWICE 8.45
NIGHTLY
4/- TO 15/6

6.15 TWICE 8.45
NIGHTLY
ALL SEATS
BOOKABLE
4/0 15/6

HIPPODROME
MAX BYGRAVES

Top: congratulating Judy Garland at the Palladium, 1951.

Bottom: Max and Judy as a 'couple of swells' at the Palace theatre, New York.

Top left: polishing my first Rolls.

Top right: how I did an act in the early fifties.

Bottom: with Lord and Lady Docker at Claridges.

Top: going to Mike Todd's party with friends, including Vera Lynn, Alma Cogan, Joe Loss, Joan Regan, Cyril Stapleton and Jimmy Henney.

Bottom: Max—with an intruder! (*BBC*)

I remember my dad
Saying "Things sure look bad
There's no jobs and we're right on the floor."

Then my mother would smile
And say, "Wait for a while
Things will get better I'm sure."

But they didn't get better
In fact they got worse
We had soup in fifty-seven different ways

And to buy food and coal
They were drawing the dole
Back in my childhood days.

It was about this time, I became aware that we were poor. When I could raise the tuppence I'd go to the Hippodrome, the cinema we patronised. If I didn't have the tuppence, I'd "bunk in"—I'd sit there and realise there were other ways of living. Fred Astaire wore tails, women had Marcel waves, motor cars we saw on the screen were *never* seen in our area.

Also, the popular films of that time were what they call "Buddy can you spare a dime" films—these had the hero, who was usually William Powell or Joel McCrea as a bum, toeing the breadlines. He landed a job; the boss's daughter fell for him; he'd have one good idea that would make the boss a few more millions and this would make the boss give work to our hero's buddies and everybody lived happy ever after.

Every punter sitting in the dark of the Hippodrome recognised him or her self. We didn't enjoy the poverty bits of the film; we knew all that. We liked it when William Powell discarded his hobo's clothes and became the suave man about town who showed those millionaires how to live.

Very few of us kids could stand love scenes. If we happened to "bunk in" for a Garbo or Myrna Loy film and they started a love scene that had kissing and tears, all the kids in the cinema would groan and there'd be cries of "We want our money back!" Once, after bunking in, the projector broke down. The manager, whose name was Mr Tremayne, walked on to the stage and announced that because we had been so tolerant waiting for the projectionist to get it right and he'd failed, we would have our money refunded if we showed our half tickets at the pay box. On this particular night, a friend named Johnnie MacDonald, and myself went down on our hands and knees to find half tickets customers had dropped between the rows—we found about eight and cashed them in, this was after we had done the "bunk in".

Another reminder that we were not like those others "Up West!" was the radio. The babble of voices and the tinkle of champagne glasses as Ambrose and his Orchestra played music from the Mayfair Hotel, reminded us of our station in life.

On a radio set that had a high tension battery and an accumulator that had to be charged every four or five days at the local sweet-shop, we heard cultured voices discussing things like how to grow rhododendrons. My father would sit there gazing at his six daffodils in the two window boxes, digesting every word. His theory was that if it worked with rhododendrons, it would work with daffodils. He could never really understand why they only lasted a few weeks and the rhodas in the park went on till autumn.

We all sat down in a circle round the speaker for Henry Hall. Nobody spoke and Henry would MC. He would introduce his guests and we would conjure up our own images. It was amazing how the image didn't always match the voices. I once heard a very cultured gentleman named Gordon Harker being interviewed. In my image, I saw him as a sort of Rex Harrison—I was shocked to see he was a small ferret-faced man, balding and stooped. We all thought he was great as a Cockney but in the past few years, since I have watched some of his old films on television, I realise that his Cockney was not accurate. It was theatre Cockney, the sort Stanley Holloway uses. It may pass for the Northerners and Americans but it isn't the Cockney I knew. Michael Caine has the only good true accent I have ever heard—I guess because he was brought up not too far from me. Graham Moffett who appeared with Will Hay in nearly all his films was another good Cockney.

My brother Harry and my four sisters were always being told by my father to "talk proper". I remember once asking my mother how to spell "jaw"—there was a discussion on whether it was J-O-R or J-O-R-E. I was writing a letter and had a line that read: "I hope your jaw is better." When none of us could come up with the right spelling, my mother said, "Put chin"—chin she could spell.

If you were an elder brother it was expected that you would look after your sisters. There were always stories of dirty old men getting little girls to do things for a bag of sweets. If we heard about anything like this, we would get our fathers to come quickly —if they caught the "flasher", they would give him a couple of right handers and he was usually never seen again in the district.

I can recall once seeing an old man doing this to a kid that lived in the same block as us—the little girl was staring up at him wondering what it was all about. It was on a piece of waste ground not too far from our block of flats. I was with brother Harry. Harry, who was fearless, called out to him: "Oi, you dirty old bastard—leave her alone." He told us to run off, "He was giving her some sweets and we couldn't have any." Harry was only about twelve but he went right in and pulled the little girl away and told her to go home. Then he turned round to the old man and told him he would fetch a policeman. "What for?" said Flasher. "For trying to have it up with little girls," said Harry. The old fellow took a swipe at my brother but missed. The waste ground was full of rubble—Harry reached down and picked up some half house bricks and began to throw them at him. I saw what he was doing and joined in. The two of us pelted him with these bricks as he ran off trying to button his flies at the same time.

As we got into the open, there were a couple of ladies gossiping with two prams laden with washing. One of them shouted: "Leave that old man alone, he ain't doing nothing to you!" There was no way we could tell them we had caught him doing what he was doing; it was *us* at fault for picking on *him*.

A few days later, one of the ladies told my father we had been throwing stones at an old man. When we got in from school, my father asked us why we had picked on an old man to stone. Harry told him that we had found him with this girl who lived above us, "Playing with his private"—there was no other way we could put it, as my father detested swearing or bad words. There was a shocked silence and no more was said.

About an hour later, my father told us he was going for a walk and we were welcome to come. We enjoyed walking with him. On this particular jaunt, he took us into Clees sweetshop and bought us a penn'orth of sweets each. This was a rare treat from him as pennies were very precious, also he walked with both his arms on our shoulders the sort of way a proud father does. I think he was rather pleased we did the stoning.

If we had a "difference" with another kid of same age, weight and intelligence, it would be fought out with bare knuckles in the street behind the school.

As soon as there was "a fight" announced, it would be round the school in no time then, immediately the bell went, those in "the know" would slope off to the spot where all fights were held. The other kids would then form a ring, the two contestants would meet in the middle, then fight it out until one had had enough.

When the opponent "gave in", there was usually a handshake and that was the end of the grievance.

I had several fights but the one I remember most was with a kid from the same class who flicked a paper pellet at me. It hit me on the back of my neck just as I was lifting the top of my desk to look for a rubber.

I could see the kid who had done it, his name was, and still is, Johnny Crawley. I threw the rubber at him in retaliation, was seen by the teacher and got two strokes on each hand. The cane and the punishment book were great deterrents, they were both painful and humiliating and furthermore the teacher, Mr Collins, enjoyed laying it on now and again. I think it cured his frustration as a bachelor, which he was then.

Anyway, after getting four handers, I let it be known that Crawley and I would meet "at the back" to settle our difference. The whole school followed us because we were both supposed to be good with our fists and as we were in the seniors, the fight would be a "heavyweight" one.

We took our coats off, rolled up our sleeves and boxed our way through the first few minutes. The kids were like the betting crowds that frequent the boxing halls even today. "Smash him in the gob", etc., etc. Often we would fight for twenty minutes without a break. Men would sometimes stand a short distance away without interfering because we didn't use bottles or knives or coshes; it was a tournament to see who was the best. After the verdict, which everybody could witness, we usually finished up as friends.

Why I remember this particular fight with Johnny Crawley, is that about thirty-five years later I had a call from Littlewoods, the football pools people, asking me to present a cheque to the winner of the then biggest amount of money ever won on a pools coupon, £103,000.

The winner was none other than my old sparring partner, Johnny Crawley. That night, him, me and his relatives turned the Grosvenor House Hotel upside down. We drank champagne and somebody said they fancied jellied eels, so the management sent out for them.

When I gave Johnny the cheque, I cracked: "Give it to me." He came back with: "I'll fight you for it!"

The photographers and publicity boys got a great story from this particular reunion. When they asked who had won the fight, neither of us could honestly remember—we settled for a draw. Wow! £103,000 in one go! Nowadays I have to work all week for that!

Charles Atlas was a big influence in our boyhood days. This man with rippling muscles jumped out at you from a paperback, saying: "You too can have a body like mine!" There were drawings of a ninety-seven pound weakling having sand kicked in his face by a bully who went off with his girl. After the weak one had taken the Charles Atlas course, he came back and "done him up".

To look like this man, we scraped and saved to raise the half-a-crown to send for the course that could make us take on Tommy Farr or Joe Louis, if we wanted.

Part of the book advised you to eat the tender meat of steaks, chickens and certain fish—this helped to build the muscle. We couldn't afford this, so we did the next best thing, we had it concentrated—in Oxo cubes. These we dissolved in hot green water, we hoped this gave us the same protein as a pound of steak. Our mother had instructions never to throw away the water she had boiled the cabbage in, as we needed it for our body building. Even Oxo cubes became hard to get—they sold in those days at two for three ha'pence—as we used about six a day between my brother and me. It became harder and harder to find the money for these.

One late evening, there was a loud rat-tat at the door. My father opened it to find a police sergeant there.

"Do you have a son named Henry Bygraves?" he asked.

"Yes," said my old man, rather worried, imagining all sorts of dreadful things that could have happened.

"Well, he's in trouble."

"What sort of trouble?"

"He's at Tower Bridge Police Station at this moment on a charge of stealing."

"What did he steal?" asked Dad.

"Oxo cubes."

"Oh well—if that's all, I'll have to pay for them."

"You'll have a job," said the copper, "He's stolen eighteen thousand of them!"

The full story was that one of the local villains who drove a horse and cart for E. Wells, the haulage firm, had taken my brother out for the day as mate. He had arranged for Harry to take the fully loaded horse and cart to a street a short distance away and load

39

the Oxo cubes on to another horse and cart. The driver would be in a cafe that was "a good pull up for carmen". He would drink his tea slowly while the "job" was going on. After he had given the thief plenty of time to shift the load, he would leave the cafe and raise the alarm. He hoped to search the streets nearby, find his horse and cart with no load, report it to the police, tell his employers he had been hijacked and lost his load, and later on he would share the spoils with his accomplice. Harry was the fall guy. After he had helped to unload he was to disappear. But things had gone wrong, he had been seen, caught, and was now at Tower Bridge Police Station.

My father put his hat and coat on, then left to go to the station. Harry was charged and told he would be given a date to appear before the magistrate, Mrs Campion, who presided over the juvenile court.

Tower Bridge Police Station has six or seven stone steps outside. When my brother and father got outside, my father in a temper because of the disgrace, hit Harry and knocked him down the steps. Harry picked himself up and ran all the way home, he got into bed crying helplessly, I could feel his body shaking with misery as he got in beside me.

When my father got home, he yanked him from the bed and gave him another beating. After that the two of us lay there crying, cradled in each other's arms. Why I was crying I don't know because I hadn't been touched. Only sleep brought that awful day to an end.

Next morning, Harry complained of this terrible pain in his face. My mother took him to St Olave's Hospital where an X-ray showed that his jaw had been broken. He was operated on and was kept in for several weeks. I can remember my father crying quite openly when he knew what he had done.

He suggested I write to Harry and put in the letter that dad was sorry for what he did. I finished the letter saying: ". . . I hope your *chin* is better."

Harry was put on probation for two years, the driver of the horse and cart was sent to Wormwood Scrubs for three months, and my father never hit one of us again from that day.

There was Elsie and Doris
Marlene and Maurice
Back in my childhood days.

There was Chesney and Bud
And the great Lobby Lud
Back in my childhood days.

On the cinema screen
All the sirens were seen
Jean Harlow had the most familiar face,

Gary Cooper was good
But George Raft was a hood
Back in my childhood days.

With the few shillings profit I made at shoe repairing, I went to the variety theatre at the top of Deptford High Street. This was known as the New Cross Empire and there you could see Gracie Fields, Max Miller and Billy Bennett—all on the same bill. You could see them but you couldn't hear them, at least not from my seat in the balcony. I always seemed to finish up in the back row of the gods, how I never got a nose-bleed I don't know, but as I fell more and more under the spell of the atmosphere, I made an all-out effort to raise the extra coppers for a better seat.

It was from the top-line artistes who appeared there that I learned jokes. Soon I began telling my family the funny things a comedian had said, then found I could get twice the laugh if I told the same story but added some of their characteristics. For instance, Billy Bennett stood stock still with his feet at twenty-to-eight, until he came to his punch-line, and, to telegraph to his audience that the funny bit was coming up, he'd wiggle his moustache once then throw one hand up in the air, rather like Ken Dodd does today. Max Miller would stand with one foot on the footlights, as if telling a confidence, then look towards the wings, as if the manager was listening to every word and would have the curtain rung down on him—should the response be doubtful, he would then tell a harmless joke and get a yell with it. His build-up to a pay-off has never really been equalled.

I learned quite a bit from watching the top liners. I learned that the people who patronised the New Cross Empire wanted their humour basic, the songs singable and the specialities breath-taking. Acts like Wilson Keppel and Betty, Max Miller, Gracie Fields and George Formby would have "Standing Room Only" boards outside, but class acts as they were known, acts like Ronald Frankau, Flotsam and Jetsam, Oliver Wakefield, and Hutch, didn't seem to have the same appeal. But I can never remember an act getting booed or ignored by this particular working-class public. If you had class it was recognisable.

43

I think the reason for this attentiveness was the fact that no act was allowed to go on for too long. Most performers can show all their tricks in fifteen minutes; over that time the acts start padding or permutating on what they have done before. The clubs have spoiled so many acts because of this—they go for quantity and not quality. Almost every top act that plays clubs is expected to be on for an hour or more. It may surprise some people to know there are hardly a dozen solo acts in the world that can go more than sixty minutes and keep an audience interested.

When I was a kid there were nine, sometimes ten, acts on a bill. Some were given seven or eight minutes, some had as little as three; even the top-of-the-bill only got fifteen. If they went over time, they were reported to head office so that they either conformed or were relegated to the smaller halls—if they didn't behave, they stopped working. It is very hard to stop an act going on when the audience are giving out generously with their applause. After all it's what they've worked most of their life for and they don't want to hear that applause cut off by the musical director going into the next act's music yet, if he doesn't exit gracefully, the next act comes on to a ragged start and that's how most of the rows start amongst members of the profession.

There are three notoriously bad weeks in show business, "the week before Christmas, the week before Easter and Sheffield." The week before Easter at the New Cross Empire was always talent spotting week—this was run by a man named Tony Gerrard who was a short, fat, round man, balding and walked with "quarter-past-nine feet". He had a gravelly voice with a northern accent. He chewed a cigar that had deep brown liquid oozing from it that he wiped on the back of his hand, then threw to the floor with a whipping sound.

The presentation was known as "Tony Gerrard's Go As You Please 'week'". It was run on the same lines as Hughie Green's *Opportunity Knocks*. The acts were auditioned the week before at the theatre, some appeared on Monday, another bunch appeared on Tuesday and a further crowd appeared on Wednesday. Acts were eliminated by audience applause. On Thursday, Friday and Saturday the cream appeared—then about ten acts would go to a final on Saturday night.

Usually, there were about half a dozen tap dancing acts, several ventriloquists, dozens of tenors singing "Because" and several tiny tots who did acrobatics—they usually won, too—oh yes, they invariably had an impressionist who did take-offs of Lionel Barrymore, Charles Boyer and James Cagney. The first prize was £25 and to give you an idea of the magnitude of that sum to me: my father would have queued up for ten weeks' dole to have made that amount.

I got a form from the box office, then filled it in—the form stated that an act had to bring their music with them. I had decided I was going to sing "It's My Mother's Birthday Today"—a real tearjerker. When I did it at parties the ladies would blubber uncontrollably so I had learned to save it for my finish. I paid sixpence for the sheet music at Woolworths and with this, in a brown paper bag, I turned up at ten o'clock on a Tuesday morning at the Empire. I had to get in a queue that went right round the theatre. At first, I thought they were queueing for a show—I didn't grasp they were there for the same reason I was.

I wore a pair of grey flannel trousers with a white "cricket" shirt and white plimsolls—I can remember standing there shivering. My hair was plastered down with half a tin of Vaseline. When we were eventually let into the theatre I have never been so pleased to get out of the cold.

My name was called and I handed my music to a pianist who looked like Hitler. He didn't even look up when I gave him my "dots". There was no rehearsal, no lights, just a dark stage and an even darker auditorium.

"Do you want the full intro or just an arpeggio?" asked the pianist, still not looking up. He could have been talking German for all I knew.

"What?" I enquired.

He decided to play the last few bars. I sang a chorus, there was no applause, nothing.

"What's your name?" said a voice from the void.

"Walter Bygraves, Sir," I said. My mother had briefed me to call Mr Gerrard "Sir".

"Alright, son, leave your name here and we'll let you know." I did this, left, then ran the two miles home to keep warm.

"What happened?" said my mother. I told her they were going to let me know.

"You won't hear another word," said my father. "They do that —when they don't want you," he muttered.

The following Friday when I got home from my paper round, my mother waved a letter from Mr Tony Gerrard telling me "I must be at the Empire five o'clock on the following Monday with full make-up and props ready to go on."

I now had all weekend to think about it. The more I thought about it, the more I thought it would be wrong to go on as I did at the audition. I wished I'd had a suit like the rest of them but I didn't own one.

At the local cinema was a film starring Wallace Beery as *The Champ*. On the fly poster there was a picture of him and a cheeky looking American kid dressed up in the "Our Gang" style; this was a look set off by Charlie Chaplin when he appeared in a movie called *The Kid*. The Kid in this case was Jackie Coogan.

With my father's cloth cap, long trousers and one brace over a ragged shirt, I was able to look a lot like him, a bit of dirt on my face completed the picture. My boyhood friend Billy Perkins had a mongrel dog that I tucked under an arm and that's how we arrived Monday evening at the Empire. I won easily. It was hard *not* to win. A boy soprano singing "It's My Mother's Birthday Today" in tattered clothes with a half starved dog—he's got to win. Even Hitler at the piano was applauding as they judged the final six.

"Come back Thursday, son," said Mr Gerrard and I walked home three feet above the ground.

When I got home from school on Thursday, my father had landed a day's casual labour at the docks. When my mother told me this, I should have been jubilant but I said, "Hope he's not wearing his cap and trousers." But he was and suddenly I had no props. I gulped my tea and ran the mile or so to the dock gates and stood bobbing up and down looking for my dad. Suddenly he appeared. "Dad—dad!" I nearly got trampled by the hundreds of dockers going home. I ran alongside him trying to make him understand, that I needed the props he was wearing, he took his cap off, put it on my head, gave me sixpence from his day's money —then disappeared, the only bare head among the throng. That, incidentally, is my favourite memory of my father.

With the sixpence I was able to get a bus and arrived a bit late but in time to go on at the Empire. By Thursday the competition had got much stronger, some of the acts were in the pro class and I just managed to get into the semi-finals on the Friday. On Friday I barely got into the finals but made it with eight other acts.

On Saturday the theatre was packed. There was great excitement and the house was filled mostly with relations and friends of the competitors.

Mr Gerrard introduced me as Master Walter Bygraves, to spin out time he talked to the contestants, who had dwindled considerably from Monday night. It was while he was talking to me, the dog, whose name was Spot, lifted his leg and did a pee. "Good job I wasn't singing Trees," cracked Mr Gerrard, "you should call him Littlewood—he likes doing his pools." The audience shrieked with laughter, they knew it was not rehearsed. A stage-hand walked on with a mop and got further laughs. Then I sang— I leaned on the song, caressed Spot and at the end I walked upstage in the spotlight, a trick I had seen Suzette Tarri do during my visits to this theatre.

I knew I was in the running for a prize. I wasn't keen on getting first prize—anything would have done—so it was in a daze I heard Mr Gerrard declare me the winner. I was pushed on from the wings with Spot, I had made a lead for him from string, we stood in the spotlight and just as Mr Gerrard was about to put the white crisp five pound notes in my hand, Spot decided to do it again— this time, as my mother has often said when she tells the story, "Big jobs"! And big jobs it was; he did it everywhere. The stage-hand reappeared with the mop, Tony Gerrard pretended to faint and I heard laughter that I had never heard before, it came in waves. I knew when I left the theatre that night all I ever wanted was to hear an audience laugh like that again. Sometimes when I am on stage and hear a real good laugh from an audience, I am back at the Empire for a brief moment or two with Spot and Mr Gerrard.

We all use t' sing
Songs recorded by Bing
Back in my childhood days.

Shirley Temple was five
We were learning to jive
Back in my childhood days.

I once saw a Zeppelin
Up in the sky
I saw the Crystal Palace all ablaze.

The gentry played polo
Amy Johnson flew solo
Back in my childhood days.

A scholar was not expected to be academically brilliant at St Joseph's, Paradise Street. They gave a degree in physics if you were able to read the label on a vinegar bottle.

I was recognised as the brain of the family because by the age of twelve I could recite Wordsworth's "Upon Westminster Bridge". I got nine out of ten for English and being able to finish the junior crossword in the *Evening News*, whilst having my tea. I didn't mention I had spent quite a long time looking up the clues on my paper round.

But my greatest claim to fame at that time was that I was the solo voice with the school choir. The singing teacher was Miss Murray who was obsessed with winning "The best school choir in South London Trophy". She would walk up and down the aisles between the desks in the classroom and put her ear six inches from your mouth listening to whether you were sharp or flat, if you were either she would grab you by the ear—march you out to the front of the class and bang the notes out on the piano. It really hurt to be tugged by the ear and was most humiliating. We were co-educational—so a snigger from the girls in the class was more embarrassing than Miss Murray's face with eyes popping, enunciating every syllable to perfect pitch. I think it must have done me some good later in life, though, because I am not the world's greatest singer, but I do sing in tune.

Miss Murray decided I was to be the soloist at a gala held one Saturday in Westminster Cathedral. The song chosen was "Jesu joy of man's desiring"—a very difficult piece even for an experienced singer, but nerve-racking for one with little or no musical training. There are some long waits and every bar has to be phrased in the hope that the singer and the accompaniment finish together.

I was kept after school by Miss Murray almost every day—she would play the accompaniment and by nodding her head as a downbeat, I would come in on cue. After about a month, the two of us became quite good—as long as I could see her nods. I became more and more confident and enjoyed this exalted position of soloist. My voice was strong and clear and Miss Murray's fingering of the keys was in sympathy.

Westminster Cathedral was packed on that Saturday afternoon —several school choirs from different parts of London were in the pews; churchmen of every order were in attendance; also, there was a judging panel from various musical colleges. Although I had butterflies in my stomach, I still felt that Miss Murray and I could give some of the others a run for their money. I looked at her sitting at the end of the pew and she winked.

A bishop or cardinal announced that we would stay in our seats and do our vocalising from there. St Joseph's was the first school to sing. First we would all sing "The Ash Grove"; next was my solo, "Jesu joy of man's desiring"; and lastly all together again for our school song "Facta—non verba!" written by the headmaster, Mr O'Connor.

Miss Murray conducted and we all sang "The Ash Grove"— there was silence as the last note trailed away in that massive mausoleum. Then Miss Murray walked to the piano. Her heels clicked in the silence. The rest of the choir were seated. I was to remain standing, ready for my solo. As she sat down to play the introduction her head disappeared behind the black upright piano. I had never sung the song without being conducted by Miss Murray's nodding head, and now I couldn't see her. I knew I couldn't judge those interminable bars of music—what could I do? I did the first bit of dramatic acting of my career. The introduction to "Jesu" is very long, I guess it's half a minute or so. As the first note sounded I went into a trance and, with eyes closed tight and hands clasped in prayer, I left the pew and walked towards the piano. All eyes had been on the animated figure of Miss Murray but now there were two people moving and I could feel all eyes on me as I stood in very much the same way as I imagine Bernadette must have stood for the Lourdes visitation.

I opened my eyes to see Miss Murray's head go down and rendered the entire piece gazing at Miss Murray. I think if it had been right to applaud, we would have got an ovation then. Over the last few bars, which are solo piano, I walked back to my seat. It was a good theatrical move and none of the panel had really noticed I had gone against the instructions laid down by the referee that we were to sing where we were—at least, if they had, nobody mentioned it.

It was going home on the tram later with the prize that Miss Murray asked me why I had left the pew. "I heard a voice," I lied ... "I heard a voice ... I think it was St Joseph ... saying 'Don't let my school down'." I got an old fashioned look from Miss Murray but she accepted it. Actually, the voice I heard said: "Wally, if you don't do something quick, you're going to look a right twerp!"

About this time, I got "worms". After about ten weeks with no sign of them leaving me, I was beginning to look like a skeleton—my bones poked through my skin and I was referred to as "Skinny Wally". It was a great source of amusement to my friends—a district nurse came daily to give me enemas, but they did no good and eventually, I was put in the local hospital. They used all manner of personal atrocities to rid me of these worms—the worm-cakes were the worst. Eventually, the hospital won and I was discharged weighing not much more than a damp rag. I was sent to a convalescent home at Ramsgate in Kent. It was the Convent of the Holy Cross, run by nuns. Here they taught young scholars to be gentlemen. There were tennis courts, a rugby pitch, gymnasium and a curriculum that took in a whole lot more than St Joseph's. The type of boy there came from a middle- or upper-class family. I was quite out of my depth for the first few weeks, but, boys being boys, I was soon one of them and because of the weight I had lost I got the name "Beanpole". Another boy had arrived with me. He was from the same district as myself. His name was Denis O'Connor and he had been down with yellow jaundice so he got the name "Chinaman". For the next three months we were great buddies, him short and yellow, me tall and pale—we were also known as "The Bermondsey Boys".

We traded confidences with each other and found that we both fancied Nurse McNally—she was an Irish nurse with big boobs, aged about twenty-four. Although we were only twelve years old, we had thoughts about her that we could never tell to our mothers.

She had a high colour, dazzling smile and laughing eyes—all I had to do was smell the disinfectant on her and I would be like a pup on heat. Just to hear the rustle of her starched apron in the dormitory after "lights-out" would make my hands dart right under the sheets.

There were approximately seventy boys and most of those over the age of twelve had their sights on her. Whenever she played tennis, the court suddenly became surrounded by young admirers —they wanted to see her run for the ball because her boobs bounced uncontrollably. She could never quite understand why we all served "easy" serves: it was no fun for the rest of us if an ace was served.

One day in the playground she noticed me rubbing the inside of my thighs which were chafed rather badly.

"What are you doing?" she asked.

"I think I must have left my legs wet when I went swimming," I said.

"You'll have to get something for it," she said, and I thought no more about it.

That night in the dormitory, I lay awake thinking of her. Suddenly I got that whiff of disinfectant that would turn me into a young stallion. I looked up and saw her standing beside my bed.

"Come on, Beanpole—where are these chapped legs?" she whispered. I gulped, "Oh God," I thought, "she mustn't see me like this—it's indecent."

She held a large jar of zinc ointment in her hand; she was unscrewing the top, pulling the blankets and sheet back; she told me to take my pyjama trousers off. I pretended I couldn't get the knot of the cord untied.

"Don't bother," she said, "I can get to it." Without batting an eye, she proceeded to skim the zinc ointment on to her right hand, then with her left she lifted open the fly of the pyjamas; she then rubbed the ointment gently on the inside of both legs; she paid no attention to my "condition".

As she covered me up she whispered, so as none of the other boys who might be awake could hear, "I hope you'll think of this next time you're in the confessional box."

Try as I might, when I went to confession I could never get round to telling the priest I'd had bad thoughts about Nurse McNally. I told Denis and all he said was, "You 'orny git!"

After about four months I left the convent to go back to Rotherhithe and the two rooms we still lived in. After having a bed to myself with clean sheets, hot water to bathe in every night and four gorgeous meals a day, I was now back sharing a single bed with my brother and grandfather. We had no sheets, just rough blankets and if it got very cold we put our father's overcoat over the blankets. My three sisters shared the other bed in the same room—my parents slept in the other room with the latest baby.

I had been taught to say "please" and "thank you", to open doors for ladies and do all the gentlemanly things that were not done in our environment. After a few days of this, my father asked me if I had become a "nancy boy".

In a week or so I lost all the polish I had acquired at Ramsgate and was back to the lingo of the buildings. I had become strong, had a good physique and was ready for the factory. I was almost certain to be sent to work. I couldn't wait for my fourteenth birthday so as I could finish school. A career in the entertainment business was the last thought in my mind. All I could envisage was a job at the docks, marrying one of a dozen girls about my own age who lived in the buildings and finishing fifty years later in the same flat we might be lucky enough to get from the council.

I look back at life "in the buildings" at the age of fourteen. It may read as if my life was one load of wallops and poverty. Let me put it right if you think that. I can hardly remember a day that wasn't lived to the full.

I was never bored. I can never remember sauntering into the flat saying, "I can't find anything to do." I lived every minute of every hour of every day. We got a great deal of love handed out and a lot of cuddles. It seems to me that cuddles are the greatest thing you can give to a child—not the ones that embarrass them but the private ones, the ones that let them know they are really wanted.

I was chastised when I did wrong. I respected my parents then and respected them later. There was a great deal of the Victorian parent in them but somehow it worked.

We respected our teachers. They arrived at school clean shaven, neat and clean and taught us that one about "cleanliness being next to Godliness".

I recently watched a march of student teachers near Hyde Park. They were striking for more pay. I cannot imagine a class having respect for many of them. The men were bearded and they looked dirty, slovenly and stupid. I may be wrong about this—maybe they get results that way—but in the last ten years I have noticed there isn't the grit there that ours seemed to have.

I know two young teachers personally. One "gypped" me out of some money I lent him, the other spends all his time thumbing through *Playboy* and *Men Only*. Neither of them have the "go" that our masters had. I mean it when I say if a new master arrived at our school with two ears, we all thought he must be a poof.

Education is a good thing. On two occasions in life I have been "twisted" out of large sums of money—once for nearly £1,000 and quite recently for £17,500—on both occasions it was by people with good education. The one that took me for £17,500 was caught and went to prison for eighteen months. In the witness box a bishop, a school principal, and various dignitaries pleaded for this wayward slip. After a year, he was out again. That's not bad is it? A year in stir for £17,500—that's more than most fellows come out with after fifty years of hard work. Maybe crime doesn't pay—but the hours are good.

I was taught to be honourable, to fight fair, not to be a mug and have a code of honour you stuck to. I hope I have done just that.

I was, and still am, cowardly about sickness—if a person is sick I will do my utmost to avoid visiting them in hospital or sick bed. I get crotchety over people coughing. When I am laid up with a cold I don't like visitors. I just want to shake it off and get back in action. I never take pills and will even shrink from an aspirin for a headache. I would rather walk in the fresh air until it has gone.

This was all part of the education I got as a kid. I can't do much about it; it's what I was taught and what I practised.

I was brought up fairly strictly as a Catholic. I am not a good one but I get the needle if people knock it too much. Then I usually find myself defending it to the full.

So now, at fourteen, equipped with good health, a sense of humour, absolutely nothing to lose, I set out to face the adult world.

The first job I was sent after was as a page boy at the Savoy Hotel in the Strand. The labour exchange I reported to gave me a green card with Savoy Hotel scrawled across it. In my very first suit with long trousers, hair held in place with Vaseline, I stood gazing at the shining chrome above the entrance. The taxis kept coming and going; Rolls Royces and Daimlers kept dropping ladies in mink and gentlemen in astrakan. I stood watching a scene I had only witnessed from a seat in the cinema. I suddenly saw a lady having difficulty opening a taxi door. I rushed forward and helped her, she thanked me, paid the driver, then turned round and gave me the change which was ninepence. I looked at the money in my hand

and thought, "This is the job for me." A few tips like this and it wouldn't be long before I had my own Daimler. As I was thinking this, a voice said, "What are you doing?" It was the commissionaire and it was obvious he wasn't pleased at me getting a tip that he should have got. "I've come for a job here," I said. "Round the back!" he yelled. He jerked his thumb and repeated, "Round the back!"

I walked in the direction he had pointed which was down Savoy Hill. I saw a sign which said: Savoy Hotel—Staff. I gave the card to a timekeeper sitting there. He looked at it and laughed. "You're too bloody big for a page boy!" He was a replica of Gordon Harker and somebody must have told him he was as great a wit as that wonderful character actor. "You'd make a bloody good lamplighter." He went on, "Here, pull this." He put out his hand with one forefinger extended. "Go on, pull it—don't be afraid." I took the finger and as I pulled he broke wind—he was helpless with laughter. "I'll bet you've never seen that one before," he guffawed. It half crossed my mind to give him a belt on the chin and then run, but what could I have told them at the labour exchange? My very first job and here I am with a jester who doesn't really care whether I work or not.

"Don't they use tall boys for running messages or errands?" I asked. "Can you run?" he said all seriously. I nodded, he lifted his leg and did the same again but twice as loud and twice as long. "Well, run after that!" He thought this was a great joke and wiped tears from his eyes with the back of his hand. He seemed to like me because I was laughing at all this—I was only laughing to humour him. When nine of you live together in two rooms, you hear a lot of that, and what I had heard would have made him envious.

He became all serious. "Hang on, son." He dialled something on a telephone, then said something to somebody at the other end. He then went back to his *Sporting Life*. Now and again he would lift one cheek off his wicker chair to trumpet like a bull elephant.

A man looking very much like Franklin Pangbourne, the famous Hollywood butler, appeared. "Card," he said, snapping his fingers. I gave him my green card with words to the effect that the bearer seeks a position as page boy, etc., etc. He looked at the card, then looked at me, scribbled something on the card, thrust it back in my hand and was gone. I looked at what he had written—there were two words "TOO TALL". The timekeeper got up, took the card from my hand, looked at the words and said: "There—what did I tell yer—you're too tall!" He then lifted his leg, did his impression of somebody ripping a sheet of calico and went back to his paper. I got the tram back home.

Incidentally, there is an end to this story. Thirty-odd years later, I was booked to appear in cabaret at the Savoy. My fee was £4,000 per week. Remembering the days of the commissionaire and the ninepence tip I got from the lady in the cab, I drove to the front entrance in my newly delivered white Rolls Royce Silver Shadow, all brightly polished. The commissionaire, dressed exactly like the one I had seen all those years ago, opened the door of MB 1 with a big salute. He recognised me and said: "Hello, Mister Max. What are you doing here?" "I'm here for the next three weeks— I'm appearing in cabaret." "Oh," he said, "*round the back*!" I half expected to see the same timekeeper when I walked in the staff entrance but he wasn't there—he'd gone—like the wind!

The second job I was sent for, I got. This was with an advertising agency known as W. S. Crawford. Their offices were at 233 High Holborn, just two doors from the Holborn Empire. I was employed as a messenger boy. It was my job to run copy to newspaper offices up and down Fleet Street and to city editors' offices in the City. It was a clean job and I got quite a lot of tips. The job was from 9 am to 6 pm with an hour for lunch. Most lunch hours were spent with sandwiches that were eaten in Lincoln's Inn Fields, a park at the back of the Law Courts, looking at photographs of the variety artistes appearing at the Holborn Empire. If I made enough tips I spent them up in the gods watching the acts there, still not realising I was watching members of the profession I would one day meet and a business that would make me a very rich man.

My most vivid memory of my days at the Holborn Empire is a newspaper seller who sold only the *Daily Telegraph*. He had a peaked cap with *Daily Telegraph* on it and an overcoat with silver buttons. He was a man of about fifty who became most interested in me. One of my jobs was to get a *Telegraph* each day for Sir William Crawford, the boss of the firm, and leave it on his desk. This I bought from the vendor I was telling you about. One day, he asked me what my hobbies were. I mentioned among other things that I liked going to the Empire. "Why don't we go together one night —I'll treat you," he said. "OK," I said, "any time you like." We fixed a night during the week.

On the night, he turned up in a pinstripe suit, grey hair neatly brushed and looking very prosperous. He bought two back stalls tickets and the show began. I leaned forward, as I always did, to enjoy it, then, half way through the first half, I felt his hand on my knee. I smiled and thought what a friendly man this is. When he squeezed a little harder, I winked at him to let him know I was enjoying the show as much as he was, only he wasn't looking at the show, he was looking at me. Not only that, his hand was getting higher and he was breathing heavier. There was something very foreign in this behaviour. I had never been warned about this at home and I didn't know how to handle it. I had been told about "nancy boys" but I didn't know anything about normal masculine-looking men that liked young chaps.

I sat there, enjoying the show less and less. My mind was occupied with how I was going to wriggle out of this affair. A fourteen-year-old boy and a fifty-year-old man—I could hear alarm bells telling me to get out, but I didn't know how.

Eventually, the curtain came down and he helped me on with my coat. "It's not late," he said, "you can come back to my place and we'll have a nice cup of cocoa." We left the theatre and he held my arm like a man does a woman's. "Where do you live?" "Only over at Lambeth," he said, "we can get a tram." He walked me down the subway at Kingsway and as we stood there he gazed at me, then said: "You are a very handsome young man." I thought "Christ—how do I lose him?"

A tram came rumbling down the subway and we boarded it, he asked the conductor for two tickets to Lambeth. We clanked towards Westminster Bridge. In a few more stops I could see myself ending up in a real mess. Even though I didn't know what was going to happen, I knew it wasn't right. He was making idle conversation and I was being polite and gay—he must have misinterpreted that "gay" bit because his eyes were shining like two new sixpences in a sweep's earholes.

As we stopped at Westminster Bridge, I saw the loveliest sight I could possibly have seen. There, illuminated by the light of the tram, stood my father—he had been to see a boxing tournament and was on his way home. "Dad!" I shouted. Like a rocket I left the tram with a loud "good night" to the newspaper seller. We got a 68 tram to Rotherhithe and I clung to him all the way home. "Don't do that," he said, "people will think you're a 'nancy boy'." The newspaper seller was most unfriendly next morning. His investment had gone awry so he completely ignored me. From then on I bought the *Daily Telegraph* from the kiosk owned by W. H. Smith.

If my brother or myself got out of hand, my mother only had to say "I'm telling your father" and we'd become lambs. She never did tell him and spent a great deal of time protecting us but sometimes she did report us. This was always over something minor, when she felt pretty sure he wouldn't give us a "right-hander".

Some nights we would all sit round while he told us stories about the war—he had spent four years in France as an infantryman and had managed to survive. Hundreds of thousands had been maimed, gassed or killed but he got through unscathed.

He made us polish our boots before we went to bed and looked behind our ears to make sure they had been washed thoroughly. He had a good sense of humour and could tell a tale very well too. Sometimes when he had us goggle-eyed at a war story, he would suddenly say "continued next week". We'd beg him to carry on but he was adamant and we'd go to bed wondering what the next episode would be like. If we didn't behave, we didn't get the continuing story, it was as simple as that.

There was no television then and we had to make our own entertainment. There was a couple who lived three or four doors from us named Dempsey. They lived in two rooms, same as us, but they had *fourteen* children. Like I said—you had to make your own entertainment.

My mother pawned everything to make ends meet—sheets, coats, shoes—anything she could pledge. She would usually pawn on a Monday and try to redeem the following Friday when my father drew his dole. If it wasn't needed or we could make do without, she'd leave it for another week and let the interest accrue.

Mondays were always the same—my mother would go to "the pawn" about nine o'clock, get a few shillings for whatever she pawned, then she'd put all the family wash on a pram, usually with the youngest wedged up the back and go to the baths. Here she got lots of hot water and a large bar of Sunlight soap, all for threepence. Then she'd scrub the lot on one of the large scrubbing boards provided. After all this back-breaking work, she'd put the lot through a "wringer". If the weather was fine, she'd hang the wet things out in the square, if it was raining they'd have to hang indoors, anywhere as long as they dried out. Then somebody invented the bagwash: for about ninepence you could have twenty-eight pounds of clothes laundered and half dried. It was my job to go to the shop and carry this load home. By the time I got it off my back all my own clothes were as wet as those in the bag. How I didn't finish up with rheumatism I'll never know.

One Monday my mother asked me to take the wash to the shop on my way to work. I was very proud of a bright red shirt I had. It was not in the bag and yet it was soiled—I undid the bag and threw it in. One of the rules of the laundry was not to include colours that ran but I didn't think of this.

When we got the wash back the following Saturday, everything was pink—my sister's confirmation frock was pink, underpants, cricket shirts, white collars that we fixed on with front and back studs were pink and so was my ear after my father had clipped it for my stupidity.

Working at W. S. Crawford put me in contact with a whole new world—I would be up and down Fleet Street every day, delivering copy and picking up proofs. I would go into the large offices of the *Daily Express*, *Sunday Times* and the smaller offices of the *Sheffield Star*, *Winchester Evening News* and various others.

There is something about a newspaper office that is hard to find elsewhere—the staff are usually sharp-eyed, aware and cynical—I think it rubs off from the upper offices. The only other business that compares with this is television, but of course TV wasn't going then, so I found the newspaper world fascinating.

One of the dreariest offices I had to go to belonged to a defunct paper called the *Daily Herald*—this was in Long Acre, quite near Covent Garden. One of the gimmicks they used to sell copies was free insurance—have a copy every day and they insured you for death, broken legs, factory accidents, etc.

There was a Fagin-like character that took the copy from us and gave us proofs. One day he buttonholed me and asked if I took the *Daily Herald*. I told him my dad sometimes bought it, so he gave me a form to take home and get my father to fill it in. He was to buy the *Herald* each day and he would have the whole family insured free. I took the form home and my father filled it in, giving the name of his newsagent, particulars of next of kin, etc.

I took it again to Fagin the following day. He was delighted because he was obviously on a commission. His crooked face was beaming all over. He assured me I was now fully insured and we would be getting our policy during the next few days. I thanked him and walked out into Long Acre with my proof copies and blocks in my arms. Some other messenger boy had left his bicycle wheel sticking out into the entrance. I walked into it, went arse over head, and broke my right arm.

A kindly old gentleman walked me down to Charing Cross Hospital where I was given an anaesthetic and came to with my arm swathed in plaster. The nurse put it in a sling for me. When I got home my mother asked me what happened. I told her, she said: "You ought to be more careful." My father said: "Nice to have you with us in the cast," and my brother said: "I hope you aren't going to whack me with that in bed." That was all the sympathy I got.

The next day I walked into the *Daily Herald* office without the sling and said to Fagin, "Did the form go through alright?" "Oh yes," he said. I showed him my plaster covered arm: "Well, I've come to make a claim." His face was a study. A few weeks later the insurance company paid me £5 and I bought a bike.

My father was still very interested in boxing and would scan the sports pages at the public library for news of the fight world. Most of his friends were ex-pugilists, they were very kind to us kids, always handing us pocket money and ruffling our hair. There was a look about them that made them seem to come from the same family—puffed eyes, thick lips and ears that resembled large rock-cakes. The more knocked about they looked, the more respect they seemed to get.

One of these ex-fighters was a man named Harry Lewis, a Jewish tailor's son. He had a business in Petticoat Lane with his father. He had served in the same regiment as my dad and they were always glad to see each other. It was a great treat to "go down the Lane" on a Sunday morning and see the crowds—we didn't see as many people as that even at a football match. I found it great fun to be pushed and jostled. I'd watch and enjoy the "salesmen" joking and cajoling the public to buy.

Harry Lewis had a great partnership going with his father. Out-side the shop, nine or ten feet up, were secondhand men's suits with no prices on. A customer would come along and start browsing. Harry wore an enormous deaf-aid with the wire hanging so it was obvious to all he was hard of hearing. "Can I help you, sir?" he'd boom—he could hear as well as anybody but he'd cup his ear to catch what the customer was saying. The person would usually point to a suit and ready to haggle he'd say, "How much?" The suit was probably worth about ten shillings but Harry would shout to his father at the back of the shop: "Dad—how much for the brown pinstripe double breasted?" Back came his father's voice that could be heard at both ends of the lane: "Thirty shillings." "How much?" Harry would say, to make sure the customer had heard "thirty", then he'd turn to let the customer get a good look at his deaf-aid and say to the mug: "Thirteen shillings."

The punter usually couldn't get the money out of his pocket quick enough and get away with the suit before the mistake was discovered. He sold a lot of secondhand suits like that. It was about the only time my father ever condoned "fiddling". It was a great source of amusement to him.

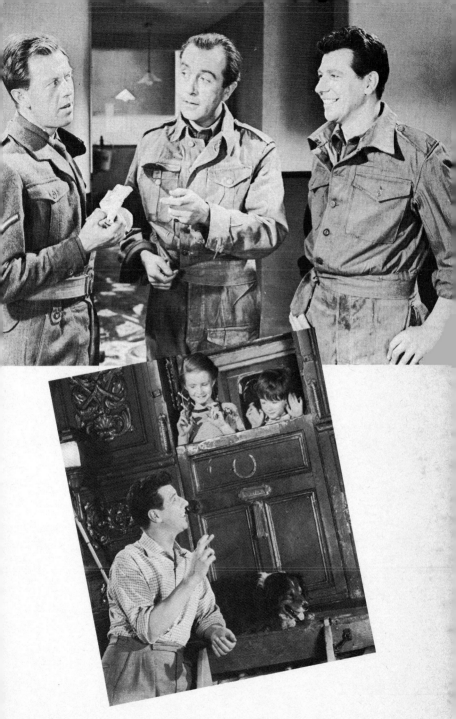

Top: first starring role in the title part of **Charley Moon** with Michael Medwin and Dennis Price.

Bottom: with seven-year-old Jane Asher, also in **Charley Moon.**

Top: as a schoolmaster in **Spare the Rod** (1961).

Bottom: a word of praise from the master, Noël Coward.

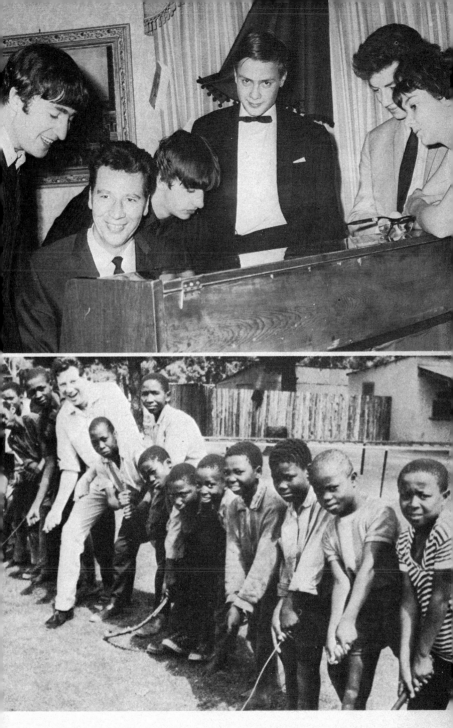

Top: John Lennon and Ringo join me for a singalong.

Bottom: a line-up of caddies in South Africa (1966).

Christine's wedding day,
with guests Cliff Michelmore, Eric Sykes and Harry Secombe.

Top: Sir Laurence Olivier, Roger Moore and myself making a record.

Bottom: congratulations from Stanley Matthews on being made a Wate Rat. Tommy Trinder looks on.

Top: Hattie Jacques recalls a funny incident for Eamonn Andrews. (*BBC*)

Bottom: one of the first entertainers to
perform to coloured audiences in South Africa.

A word with Her Majesty.
Peter Sellers, Frank Ifield and Arthur Haynes look on.

Blossom and I arrive in Honolulu.

Ten fags were fourpence
A pint cost the same
Back in my childhood days.

Rhubarb and custard
Corned beef and mustard
Back in my childhood days.

Liquorice and lollipops
Sherbert and acid drops
And salad but without the mayonnaise.

We use t' go hiking
We use t' go biking
Back in my childhood days.

In 1937 I was fifteen. There was great unrest in Europe and quietly we started to mobilise. Work became more plentiful. My father was working almost every day, every week. My mother was going out to work at a gas mask factory somewhere up near London Bridge. The eldest of us kids, Harry, me and Lil, were all going to work too.

We still lived in the same two rooms. My father was continually writing letters to the council for some better accommodation, but there was none. It had been bad enough living in two rooms when we were children but now we were five adults and three children. The only respite we got was when our grandfather moved into a room at Rowton House, Kings Cross.

Most of the summer days I spent on my bicycle. I loved to cycle into the hop-field districts of Kent. On weekends we'd leave London with our camping gear and bike the thirty-odd miles to places with names like Paddock Wood, Goudhurst and West Malling. We'd pitch our tents in any old field and sleep peacefully alone in a sleeping bag. After the way we slept at home, it was sheer luxury. We were healthy and suntanned and very fit, apart from the cycle exercise we were all keep-fit addicts and most of us owned chest expanders or Indian clubs. We were all good or fair swimmers and would often swim the breadth of the Thames at Wapping.

Some Sundays we'd cycle to a transport cafe at Swanley in Kent, about twenty miles away, to listen to a juke-box. This big chrome and walnut machine with the coloured lights round it was to me an electronic wonder. To see the arm come out, pick up a 78 rpm record, lay it gently on the turntable and then hear the voice of Bing Crosby for three or four minutes over the speaker, all for a penny, was the greatest value I knew.

Sometimes I would play a shillingsworth, then cycle the twenty miles back home again in the same evening, broke. It was the first juke-box I had ever seen and I would make every endeavour to hear it and watch it work.

I can never think of that journey without thinking of an incident that happened on the Sidcup By-Pass, the road we used to get to Swanley.

There was a big traffic jam at a roundabout, it was being caused by a lady learner driver who was backing, shooting forward, reversing and making no progress whatsoever. Behind was a police car with a big black speaker mounted on top. This was probably unnerving the poor lady in the driver's seat because she seemed to be making such a mess of it all. Behind, motorists were tooting horns and shouting to her.

Suddenly, a voice over the speaker of the police car quelled the irate drivers by saying: "Alright, ladies and gentlemen—be a little tolerant—we were all learners at one time!" The horn blowing stopped immediately, as it did, the woman backed right into the police car; the traffic cop had left his microphone switched on and the next remark came over loud and clear: "What's the silly cow done now?"

During the winter months, I kept going to evening classes—I had taken up carpentry and enjoyed it so much I tried to give shoe repairing a miss but of course shoe repairing was more lucrative. Most of the things made in carpentry were accepted as gifts—you can't charge your mother if you make her a pastry board, or your father for a pipe-rack. I made both these items, I don't know why, my mother never made pastry and my father was a non-smoker.

"BACK IN MY YOUNG MAN'S DAYS"

There was Hitler and Goering
And the whole world was warring
Back in my young man's days.

Road blocks and pylons
Black Market nylons
Back in my young man's days.

Hokey Koke at the Palais
Gracie Fields singing "Sally"
Glen Miller and the Ink-Spots were the craze.

Soldiers and ATS
Home guard in battledress
Back in my young man's days.

When the war came, the firm of W. S. Crawford closed down, newspapers had been reduced to a few pages; there was little advertising; neon lighting was switched off and I was out of work.

There was a great demand for building-trade workers so I decided to become a carpenter and my first job was for F. G. Minter. I helped to build the air raid shelters for Crosse & Blackwell, a canned food firm in Bermondsey.

For the first few months I was tea-boy. The workmen on the site gave me a penny, the cost of a cup of tea then, with a big bucket I'd go to the cafe to get it filled—they'd bring their mugs and I would fill them from a ladle. The cost of filling this bucket was about two shillings from the cafe but then I made an arrangement with an aunt who lived near the factory gate—she'd buy half a pound of Brooke Bond tea for fourpence, half pound of sugar for twopence, milk was one and a half pence a pint, so for sevenpence ha'penny old money, we'd have a profit of roughly one and fourpence twice a day. I split it with her, it helped to supplement my meagre apprentice wage, and gave her almost as much as she was getting from a widow's pension. Alas, the job ended and I was sent to another one in Lewisham, South London.

We had been getting some bad air raids lately. My job at the time was to mend some rather large joists that were supporting a slate roof over a house. I was busy working when the siren alert started. There had been many of these in the past so I wasn't bothered too much. I looked up from the roof and saw several black specks in the sky. They were German bombers. The ack-ack was bursting all over but it didn't seem to stop their progress. I watched for a while then got the greatest shock: about one hundred yards down the road a bomb landed. I left the roof where I was sprawled and came down with a thud. I began to slither towards the guttering and just managed to grip the edge of the ladder I had used to get up to the roof. The ladder stopped my descent but I had toppled it and was falling with the ladder—luckily, I fell into a large privet hedge below and although bruised and badly shaken, I was alright.

After falling about thirty feet, the woman who owned the house came out, looked at the mess that was her privet hedge and said to me: "You should have been down the shelter."

I didn't bother to go up on the roof again—I went to a cafe for some lunch. As I drank a cup of tea, I noticed several buses with the words "Yorkshire Grey" on the front—this was a large pub in Eltham that had been taken over to give medical examinations to armed forces volunteers.

I made up my mind there and then to join the RAF. I paid for my tea, caught the next bus to the Yorkshire Grey, had an examination, was passed A1 and three days later got my papers to report to RAF Cardington. I was seventeen and a half.

I was only a pup
But I went and joined up
Back in my young man's days.

In my uniform blue
I was one of the "few"
Back in my young man's days.

Buttons of brass
A service gas mask
Brylcreem on my hair
I was away

Chatting up all the birds
It was too good for words
Back in my young man's days.

I didn't have the heart to tell my mother that I had joined up—
I left a note on the mantelpiece, telling both my mum and dad that
I had joined the Royal Air Force. I was told that when she read it,
she cried and through her tears said: "What can he do in the
RAF? He can't drive an aeroplane."

I had tried to pass as air crew but my eyesight let me down so I
had to go as a fitter on the airframes.

On my first evening in the RAF I went to the NAAFI with
several other fellows who had just joined. We were still in civvies,
it was obvious from the style of our clothes who were well-to-do
and who were like myself.

A sergeant walked on to the stage where a pianist was trying to
play "In the Mood". He blew a short blast on a whistle and we
were all attentive while he told us what we would be doing next
day: drawing our kit, packing our civilian clothes up to send home,
be issued with ration cards to buy cigarettes, soap, chocolate, etc.
He then said we were expected to make our own entertainment and
asked if there were any new arrivals who had been entertainers
before joining—one fellow put his hand up and said he sang with
D'Oyle Carte Opera. He was called on the stage and sang "Bless
this House"; he sang it very well too. When the sergeant asked for
any more volunteers, I put my hand up: "I can do an impersona-
tion of Max Miller." He said, "Come on then." With a pint of
NAAFI beer inside me, I went into Max Miller's routine that I had
done at many parties back in Rotherhithe. I was well applauded
and returned to a lot of back slapping. Several of the lads thought
I was a professional, which pleased me tremendously.

Next day in the billet, because we had not learned each other's
names, I was called Max, because of the impression I had done the
night before. It stuck and I was never known as anything else after
that night. I didn't choose it, it just stuck. I moved on for square
bashing to Bridgnorth up in Shropshire with the same bunch of
fellows and although some of them found the life hard and

uncomfortable, to me, after the buildings, I felt I was in the lap of luxury.

I had a bed to myself, the food was far better than anything I had got at home, there was lots of it too. I was able to shower every day if I wanted to. What's more, I looked like everybody else. That's the good thing about being in uniform, until you speak you are all on a par. We were mostly all getting the same pay too, so I didn't find any hardship.

One day I was given an evening pass that would allow me outside the camp from "after duty" until midnight. That evening, I got aboard a large lorry at the camp gates and was dumped in the High Street of Downtown Bridgnorth—the swinging nightlife was made up of a YMCA, a Toc H, a cinema that was closed and a few pubs that were also closed because of a beer shortage. With a civilian gas mask (this came in a brown cardboard box with string to go round your shoulder) and a brand new uniform, I wandered several times up and down the High Street. The regular airmen with a few years' service would ridicule us "rookies" no end. A group of them passed me on this evening. One of them eyed the civvy gas mask box and said, "Oi—let your budgerigar loose." There was nothing to do so I decided to walk back to camp rather than wait the few hours for the return of the lorry that brought us in.

It was dusk when I left the town. The camp was a couple of miles away. When I was about a mile from the camp, I could see lights in the billets and vehicles moving, the road seemed a long way round so I decided to cross a few fields towards the lights. I was doing fine but of course it was getting darker, there was no moon and over in the camp the blackout rules were being rigidly carried out. All at once it was as though I was in a darkened room and I could see nothing. I stumbled against fences, climbed them and hoped I was heading in the right direction.

Quite suddenly I heard a noise which made me aware I was not alone. I stood still and tried to fathom out what it was—then all hell broke loose. I saw large white birds passing by me—they were screeching and flapping their wings—I had walked into a field full of chickens, what's more, I was standing amongst them. The noise was deafening. It was like a scene from Alfred Hitchcock's *The Birds*. I was petrified. I cannot remember being so scared before. "Oh God," I cried to myself, "Oh God." If ever I needed his help, I needed it now.

I ran and ran till I came to a hedge. For a moment a light flickered about two hundred yards away. I crossed a road and recognised the barbed wire surrounding the camp. I just wanted to be on the other side of that wire. I forced my way through, the wire ripping my brand new uniform as I went. I cut my face, my hands and my legs trying to get through the entanglement, but made it.

I signed the book at the guardroom to prove I had returned and limped to my quarters. Most of the thirty-odd fellows in the hut were asleep, I undressed quietly and took hours to drop off.

In the morning the chap in the next bed was gazing at me as if I was a freak: "What have you been doing?" He handed me a mirror. I looked and couldn't see a square inch of skin that hadn't been mutilated by the barbed wire. "You been out with a bird?" he asked. I told him what had happened but he didn't believe me. "Have you got her address?" he chided. At the wash basin in the ablutions I tried to patch up the scratches. These I didn't mind; what was worrying me was the uniform. It was almost in tatters and I had to be on parade in a short while.

It was still dark, the dawn hadn't quite broken when I went to the mess hall for breakfast. Almost everybody was telling me that I had great big rips in my uniform. I dreaded when I got on the parade ground and the flight sergeant started asking questions. Nobody had believed my story; I felt pretty sure he wouldn't. He was a dedicated man, been in for years and loved the service life. His name was Flight Sergeant English—he was a Welshman.

At the breakfast table was an airman I later became pals with, he was much older. He was thirty-six but to a seventeen-year-old thirty-six seems like seventy. Because of his age, he was excused PT and route marches. I stayed pals with him until a few years ago when he died from illness. He was the coolest romancer I knew at that time—he could charm the birds from the trees. His name was Ben Slennet.

On the parade ground we were standing stiffly to attention—because I was tall I was what they call "marker". The marker stands on a spot then the rest of the squad move up, next tallest and so on, until the line looks fairly uniform. After we had done this, we stood to attention whilst the flight sergeant checked we had shaved, polished our brass, boots, and our hair was cut to regulation length. After he gave the order for attention, he came in for inspection. He couldn't believe his eyes as he looked at me. It was a good half minute before he spoke, his eyes grew wider, he whispered: "What the hell . . ." He stopped. He had never seen anything like it in his long career. "I'm sorry, flight sergeant, I had a bit of bother." I tried to explain how I had walked into the chickens. It was making no impression whatsoever. I got more and more flustered.

Suddenly Ben Slennet, who was standing next to me, piped up, "Excuse me, flight sergeant, sir." He knew how to do it did Ben. "Excuse me, sir . . . he isn't telling the truth—I know the truth, flight sergeant." Flight Sergeant English was very curious. Without taking his eyes off my face he gave permission for Slennet to tell him what happened.

Ben, in his plausible way, said: "Well, sir, he had an evening pass and went to Bridgnorth for the night, he went into a pub there that was filled with the army, they started to take the mickey out of the RAF, saying that we couldn't do without Brylcreem and all that sort of thing. Bygraves here couldn't stand it and there was a bit of a barney." The flight sergeant's eyes began to twinkle; he rather liked the idea of somebody defending his beloved RAF.

Ben laid it on: "He took six of them on, flight sergeant—that's what they did to him. Not only that, they way-laid him on the way back, he had to get through the wire to stop himself being beaten up."

The sergeant's eyes became very tender. "Well, look boyo," he said to me, "you had better get over to the sick bay and get those scratches attended to." I could feel the pride he had in me. I looked quickly at Ben Slennet but he was gazing ahead.

When I got back from sick bay covered in iodine there was a chit on my bed signed by the flight sergeant for the stores to provide me with a new uniform.

Ben and I have gone over this story at every meeting for the last twenty-five years. Every time we have finished up laughing helplessly and toasting Flight Sergeant English, the Welshman who lived in Edinburgh. If he is alive and reads this, I hope he remembers and has as good a laugh as Ben and I have done.

After six weeks at Bridgnorth, I was sent to Weston-super-Mare to learn how to become a fitter. It was a crash course and from there I was posted to Hornchurch in Essex to join a Spitfire squadron that belonged to City of Liverpool and was known as "611". The "611" were mostly "scousers". Ben and I were the only two Cockneys in the whole squadron.

I also made friends with a kid named Harry Woods who one

78

weekend decided to get married to a girl at Fazackerley which is in Liverpool. I happened to have a weekend pass, if I had gone home it would have meant being cramped up in bed again so when he asked me to go to Liverpool to be best man, I jumped at it. I loved travelling and the journey to Liverpool had me staring wide-eyed from the windows. Having to stand in the corridor of the train for almost five hours with lots of other members of the armed forces also on leave didn't worry me one bit.

Harry had a wedding party that went on until Tuesday morning. Tuesday night we rolled back to camp, were put on a charge for being absent without leave and put in detention for fourteen days. This meant running at the double with full pack on, living alone in a cell, losing all leave and privileges, and having your pay stopped. It was an expensive weekend.

I was now eighteen and growing up very fast. Ben Slennet had "been around". I listened, fascinated, to his stories of women, gangsters and clubs he had frequented in London. He exaggerated quite a lot but it made good listening, especially in the gloomy nissen huts we were living in on the dispersal area.

Another relief from boredom was a pretty WAAF who cycled past each morning. Most of the lads would stand on the perimeter as she went by and give out with the wolf whistles. I hadn't been so excited about anybody since Nurse McNally but she never gave me a second glance.

It was at one of the camp concerts that I sang a song that was most popular at the time—the song was "If I had my way". The following morning, I went into the Mess Hall and there was the pretty WAAF who went past on the bike each day. "Hello," she said, "weren't you the fellow singing with the band?" I said I was and she asked me to write the words of "If I had my way" out at sometime. I said I would and gave them to her the following day, "Can I take you out one evening?" I asked. Gosh, I was a smooth one. We started courting. She was promoted to corporal and then to sergeant. I was still an AC2 and got the name of "Crawler" for making up to a sergeant. The only way to stop this was to get married, which we did on 12 September that year—we were both nineteen. It surprised a lot of people when I married "Blossom"; it has surprised them even more to see that we have stayed married for over thirty years, especially as I came into a business that is not famed for happy wedlock.

Blossom was born and bred in Essex. She came from a large

family: three sisters and six brothers and one living parent, her mother, who didn't care for me one bit.

Mrs Murray lived in a small flat in Romford and the first time Blossom took me to meet her was a disaster. I had never heard of seances and spiritualists, which she was very serious about. After we had met and had a cup of tea, she asked me if I believed in spirits—to be funny, I said: "Yes, if they're in a bottle." It misfired completely and I was "out" from then on.

She discouraged Blossom from going with me. She had other ideas for her daughter, whom she reckoned deserved more than an AC2 with no trade or future when the war was over.

She had another son, Alf, who was an officer in the RAF and another daughter, Barbara, with the Land Army. She had told her children that she was distantly related to Royalty—where, I've never found out.

Because it was her daughter, she went along with me coming home now and again and with each visit I found the ice breaking a little.

I found that if I "moodied" up to her, she warmed. I would tell her that her hat looked nice or a coat she wore looked elegant and she'd preen. I sometimes brought her my soap ration, or sweet ration and slowly she began to change her mind about me but it was a long process.

Blossom is a fun lover. She will join in any prank, providing nobody gets hurt. You can sell her an old bowler hat, she's so naïve sometimes. She was always nicely groomed and the RAF uniform suited her very well. She was slim with good legs, big, very big, blue-grey eyes and "wiggled" long before Marilyn Monroe came on the scene.

She had worked at a cinema before joining up and could tell more about the film world than anybody I knew at that time. She had seen *Seventh Heaven* with James Stewart and Sylvia Sydney eight times, because she was in love with James Stewart. I could always do a fair impression of Mr Stewart and sometimes in the middle of our lovemaking, I'd go into his drawl, saying things like: "Well——you kiss—er—pretty good—er—Blossom—yep—pretty good—er do you—think I—er—could have—my er—ear back!"

I was posted to Scotland, then Blossom wrote to me to say she was pregnant. The following May our first daughter Christine was born.

Blossom was living with her sister at Dagenham and when I got leave she very kindly gave us her and her husband George's room, as a sort of bridal suite. Of course, Blossom had left the service and all at once I had to provide. She got a marriage allowance but it was meagre. Now I got restless, the war was dragging on and I wanted to get demobilised and support my wife and baby—suddenly, I became concerned about my future.

What could I do? I knew I was not a brilliant scholar—I knew I had good horse sense. If the right opportunity came along I knew I could make more money than I could as a "chippy". Entertaining had not entered my head. I still treated it as a game. In my wildest dreams I never guessed that one day I would be in the millionaire class. At that moment I was more concerned about how I could make an extra ten shillings a week.

It was at Blackpool that it hit me—I had been sent there to do an advanced fitters' course. I had been appearing in an RAF concert they called "Contact". It was organised by a man named Jack Rose, who was an AC like myself. He liked the act I had got together and was fond of me as a performer, gave me lots of good hints on make-up and stage deportment, etc.

One day he asked me if I would like to appear at a theatre in Warrington—I had to stand in for an act known as Murray and Mooney. They had been booked to do a broadcast and had to drop out for the Saturday performance at the Warrington Opera House.

Jack Rose fixed me with a pass and railway warrant and off I went. I did a ten-minute act in the first and second houses. As I was getting dressed to go back to Blackpool, the manager came into the dressing room, thanked me, gave me a receipt to sign for ten pounds, which he handed to me in cash. It was the very first money I had ever earned from entertaining!

When I got back, I told Jack Rose what had happened. He said, "Don't forget you pay agent's commission." I didn't know what agent's commission was. "Sure, take it," I said. He took fifty per cent, which he assured me was the normal commission, but even with a fiver I was elated.

He got me more and more of these jobs. I was cleaning up. Bloss had never had so much money either. I was sending home sometimes five or six pounds every week. It was then that I made my mind up to be a pro. I liked this freedom from worry that money brought.

I worked hard at it, sorting out anybody that had anything to do with the footlights. From a chap named Tony Sherwood I learned to play a ukelele. Vera Lynn's brother, Roger, taught me some dance steps. Norrie Paramor, who today produces my records, accompanied me on piano. From all this work I was beginning to get a polished look. I would work the lights, paint scenery, even make clothes—anything as long as I was near the smell of the greasepaint.

I had even picked up enough experience to direct. When I was posted to an aerodrome at West Malling, I found they had no concert party. I organised one and called it "Chocks away", we performed at YMCAs, hospitals, satellites, sometimes to a dozen soldiers on a gun site, all this was on top of my normal duties as a fitter. There were nights when I had worked through until morning but I was always ready and willing to be on stage.

I did sketches, dressed up as a woman—hula girl, WAAF, charlady—I sang, I compered, I told jokes, I was loving every moment. Suddenly it was all over; it was peace time and I was a civilian again—after five years I was back to what I was the day I had joined up.

The war had been won
We'd defeated the Hun
Back in my young man's days.

Rudolph Hess use to smile
At the Nuremburg Trial
Back in my young man's days.

Mr Attlee was "in"
Winston Churchill was "out"
The lights went up in Britain with a blaze.

It was all back in "civvies"
We were workers and "skivvies"
Back in my young man's days.

Blossom had been working as a telephone operator at the Rainham, Essex, Exchange. I had managed to save nearly one hundred pounds and that's all we had. I got a grey chalk pin-stripe demob suit and went to live in the one room Blossom's sister had decorated for us in Dagenham—I was twenty-three.

I began work right away on a building contract in East Ham, London. I was earning £5 15s od per week and hated every moment. We had to help to make bomb-damaged houses habitable. It was miserable work but I stuck it for about three months.

If it rained, you were laid-off—no work, no pay. On one particular day it poured. I sat in the cafe for a while until the foreman poked his head in about midday and told us to go home. It was not much use going home as Blossom was at work, so I cleaned myself up to go for a trip up the West End.

I found myself outside the London Palladium, just about to pay ninepence to sit in the gallery, when somebody tapped me on the shoulder. It was an ex-officer, Flight Lieutenant Landau, a famous London impresario who had directed some shows I had appeared in. He asked me what I was doing and I told him. His face looked as if he was eating a sour apple. "There is a new show being done by the BBC called *They're Out*. They are auditioning this afternoon, go and have a try," he said. I was off like a shot to the Aeolian Hall in Bond Street, where I waited with about twenty others. One of them was the most nervous man I had ever seen, he kept putting his hands together as in prayer, his eyes were closed and his lips moved but no sound came from him.

Later I got to know him. He told me his name was Frankie Howerd and he was very funny. In fact he was so funny that they hardly gave us a hearing at the BBC, so enamoured were they with him, but I managed to get booked for a broadcast in a couple of weeks' time. I had managed, by phoning a few club secretaries at various British Legion and working men's clubs, to get a few dates and was making a pound or two extra. I always got re-booked and in my small way became quite a favourite on this working man's circuit.

Christine was growing into a beautiful little girl. My thoughts at that time were to be a semi-pro, who had a building job in the day, worked a couple of nights at weekends in clubs, spent some evenings with Blossom at the cinema, or if we didn't go out, have a cuddle in front of our own coal fire. But the broadcast I did for the BBC didn't let these thoughts materialise. That one broadcast was to alter my whole life.

It was heard by bandleader Jack Payne, who had turned impresario. He was about to launch a new show called *For the fun of it* starring Donald Peers. Frankie Howerd and myself were booked to appear in it, if we wanted to. For both of us it was our first show and for both of us it was a big decision.

The show was to open in Sheffield and was booked to play Moss Empires for sixteen weeks, then every week in a different major city. I was offered £15 per week and of that I had to pay £1 10s od commission back to Jack Payne's office as agent's fee. This racket I think has been stopped these days.

After a long talk with Blossom, I decided to take Jack Payne's offer and do the tour. She has never been one to stop me from doing what I want to do. Deep down she knew I liked being on a stage and getting results for the thinking I did all day long. She never complained when I went off into another world. I thought it was just going to be for sixteen weeks. By then I would have had that much more experience—it wasn't every beginner that could start his career on a number one tour. That usually came after slogging round the number threes, "the sticks" as they were called—then I hoped to come back to London, live at home and carry on doing the semi-pro work I had been doing previously. The decision hadn't been that hard to make for either of us because we still had no home and although my sister-in-law was very kind about it and never let on, I knew she would have liked our room back for her own family who were growing up. It was an advantage for them for me to be away.

So, on a day in May, I opened with the show *For the fun of it* at the Sheffield Empire. I had travelled on the train with the rest of the company. It was made up of Jean Adrienne and Eddie Leslie, a knockabout comedy duo, Art Christmas, a multi-instrumentalist, sixteen John Tiller girls, a puppeteer named Rene Strange, Frankie

Howerd, the star of the show, Donald Peers, and yours truly, whose bill matter was "creating an impression".

On the train, the touring stage manager, Bill Lyon-Shaw, told Frankie and me that if we reported to the theatre as soon as we arrived, the stage doorman would be on duty and he would give us a list of "digs"—they would cost anything between £1 10s 0d and £2 10s 0d per week, unless we "catered" for ourselves—that way we could probably get the room for just one pound.

Donald Peers had a young pianist who had done quite a bit of touring and knew the ropes, his name was Ernest Ponticelli. Ernie and me chummed up and wandered off to look up the list the doorman had given us of likely landladies. We settled for one in a back street I forget the name of, she was known as Ma Knight, one of the most naïve persons I've ever met.

She told us a story about a show that had played Sheffield a few weeks back. This show was a huge success, cashing in on the war that was still uppermost in people's minds, and called *Soldiers in Skirts*. The show had several female impersonators, most of who made no pretence about their profession during the day; they would often walk through the streets in full make-up.

This Ma Knight thought they were such a treat to have in the house. "So clean," she said to us. "Spotless, and kind—do you know, one of them was walking home here one night from a party and he saw this sailor. This poor sailor had nowhere to sleep, so he brought him home here. He said to me, Mrs Knight, he said, this poor fellow's been away to sea for four months and he can't find a hotel or YMCA, or anything, so I've brought him here because you have a bit more respect for somebody who is still serving their country." Ernie and me sat there unbelieving as she went on, "Do you know what he said?" We both shook our heads. "Let him have my bed, *I'll* sleep on the settee."

"Did he sleep on the settee?" I asked. "No," she replied. "The sailor said *he* would sleep on the settee, well they argued and then he said 'I've got a big double bed—why don't we both be comfortable' and that lovely man let that sailor share his bed for the next week, what's more, he gave me an extra ten bob for the little bit of extra washing-up I had to do."

When I got to know landladies a bit more, it occurred to me that some of them were even more stage-struck than we were. As soon as we arrived, they'd tell us about the "greats" that had stayed there.

Jimmy James, a comedian of the older school, got one of these "flash" landladies once. As he was being shown his room, she was pointing to framed pictures of stars who had stayed with her. Pointing each star out as they ascended the stairs, she'd say, "We've had Gracie Fields—Talbot O'Farrell—Josef Locke—Arthur Lucan and Kitty McShane . . ." At the top of the stairs was a print of a painting of "The Last Supper" by Leonardo da Vinci—Jimmy James pointed to it and said, "I see you've had Doctor Crock and his Crackpots." She asked him to leave.

I had shabby digs in Bradford where the landlady promised that on our next visit the place would be redecorated—she had been telling acts that for years but it was never done. She'd explain what it would be like next time we came. "I'm having all new furniture—not utility—I'm having fawn flock wallpaper—in the bay window I'm getting green crush velvet curtains and round the top I'm having a *pelvis*."

Most of them were kind old dears who did it for a few extra pounds—they took our ration books with meat, sugar, soap, etc. and did a very good job in spite of the country still being severely rationed.

I sent for Blossom and Christine to come to some of these towns with me but they never really enjoyed it. Blossom just grinned and put up with it. Half way through the tour, she found she was pregnant again.

We had managed to find a couple of rooms in Woolwich and the time we spent there was one of the most miserable I have ever known. The landlady refused to have children in the house so we had to leave my daughter Christine in the care of another sister-in-law. Blossom was growing bigger every day; there was hardly any coal; the cooker leaked gas; the rooms were like ice boxes and I think that 1947 is on record as being one of the coldest winters ever.

Anthony was born on 22 February that year at the East End Maternity Home. The people we lived with at Woolwich took pity on us and let us stay an extra month with the new-born baby but we had to leave when the month was up.

With just a few days to go, we heard we had been given a council house in Romford, Essex. We moved into 23 Thorntons Farm Avenue with four-year-old Christine and four-week-old Anthony. Our very first house and we worked like beavers to make it home. I was getting lots of work and my money had gone up considerably. I was now making £35 a week, and it came easy. The house was furnished from top to bottom. In three months I had a second-hand Anglia car. You never forget your first car number; it was GUF 650. I have MB 1 now but I find GUF 650 the easiest to remember.

Engagements were getting steadier—I was playing some "class dates" too. I had left the touring show *For the fun of it* a few months before. I found that working for Jack Payne was dead-end—he was the impresario, so naturally he wanted every act as cheap as he could get it.

One day in Leicester Square, a man with dark eyes and a good-natured smile introduced himself to me. He said he was Jock Jacobsen and the previous night he had seen my act at Chelsea Palace. He had a string of dates that he and his partner, Norman Payne, were booking for a star, who died early in what should have been a great career, named Steve Conway. He asked me if I felt like signing with his office. They handled a few "name" acts like Sam Costa and an act known as The Nitwits. I agreed to go under his banner.

A manager, to be good, has to have a lot of things going for him. He has to be liked; he has to be shrewd; he has to be straight; if he isn't, sooner or later he will be found out and it's pretty sure his client will go elsewhere. He has to be a friend, because a manager and client spend a lot of time together, travelling, in hotels and socially, and if you cannot work together there will be friction. Jock had all these qualities. His only drawback was that he wasn't in the big league; he was looking for the breaks just as much as the rest of us.

He managed to get me £50 a week. For this he got £5 commission—he probably spent that a week on phone calls, trying to "place" me. He got me in revues, pantomimes and variety dates—I did Masonics, night clubs, broadcasts and made my first record, singing with the Carrol Gibbons Band for the Parlophone label. I did a medley of Jolson songs which I think sold two copies— I bought one and Jock bought the other.

I made three films where I played the second lead to Hal Monty called *Bless 'em all* and *Skimpy in the Navy*, then a short that we finished in two days—they gave that the title *Nitwits on Parade*. I was touring all over the country. One week I'd be booked at Plymouth, the next perhaps Newcastle—all these journeys I did in the little Anglia—petrol was rationed and there were no motorways, so it was hard graft.

Most times I would give a lift to some of the company on the bill.

There was just a small boot to the Anglia and we've often been seen riding the A1 with five people and props piled high to the roof. If I did it nowadays I would be stopped on suspicion of ferrying immigrants.

Frankie Howerd had become a big star in the meantime. His broadcasts on *Variety Band Box* had been brilliant. Unfortunately his success came at the early part of his career and he finished up signing contracts that were for far less money than he was worth. He has since told me that he was duped out of thousands and thousands of pounds. Today, if he had been handled right, financially, he would have been a wealthy man. He had no wife or children to support, no house, he didn't even own a car, yet a few years after his fantastic success he was having a lean time. I am glad to say he is alright now.

Frank had introduced me to a new writer who was writing scripts for his hilarious routines; his name: Eric Sykes. We became great friends and have been ever since. Between us, we dreamed up ideas for comedy bits. I would take them into theatres I was appearing at and mould them into new routines. Gradually I was getting a lot of notice taken of me.

I had some good jokes. I did impressions of the different way different people play darts. I also did a strong impression of Al Jolson. I played piano and sang—in all, I had what the pros called a "very solid act".

We talked, ate and breathed showbusiness. We never discussed politics, religion, current affairs—nothing. We would read the show biz papers, talk of new performers, new productions, new songs and we were always waiting for something big and new to happen.

It came from a chance meeting of Jock Jacobsen and Cissie Williams, a lady who was responsible for the booking of the Moss Empires circuit. One day Jock was waiting to see her about some dates when he heard her talking to Val Parnell about a replacement for Ted Ray. Ted was appearing on the current bill at the London Palladium but had to go to do a concert in Manchester—he was committed for the following Thursday. She confessed to Jock that she knew nobody of Ted's stature that could fill this important spot.

Jock said, "Why look any further? You have a comedian who has been getting nothing but praise from every manager at every theatre he works. He is appearing at the Finsbury Park Empire, he could 'double' from there with the Palladium on Thursday."

All this took place on the Tuesday. That same evening Val Parnell and Cissie Williams came to the Finsbury Park Empire to watch me work. When they had seen me, they told Jock they were going to try me in that spot at the great London Palladium, preceding my dream girl Dorothy Lamour.

There were three shows that day at the Palladium and two at Finsbury Park. I did the first one at the Palladium and did the other four performances in relays. It made me a little giddy but at the end of the day I was assured by Val Parnell that I would be in his next presentation at that famous theatre—a few weeks later, I opened on the bill with those famous American comedians, Abbot and Costello.

A little while before Frank Sinatra had appeared there. He made a great deal of press by asking for a cup of English tea—one was brought on and he sipped it between songs. It was great public relations, and as I say, it got great publicity.

Eric and I dreamed up a bit of business where I would ask for a cup of tea and do the same but the idea was for a scruffy stagehand to bring it on, not a dolly chorus girl like Mr Sinatra had. After he had brought the tea, I would sing a ballad that was very popular at the time, "My Foolish Heart". As I stood there singing this with the tea in my hands, Eric would reappear with some milk in a bottle, then go off. A little later, he would come back with sugar, then go off and, lastly, he'd bring a spoon to stir it all. As I took the last big note of the song, he'd take the cup, drink the tea and exit. When it came for my tea drinking there would be none left. This got big laughs and the reviews were most generous—modesty forbids me from quoting what they wrote but many thought I had stopped the American invasion of performers.

Val Parnell held me over for a new bill starring Donald Peers, who was having new life as a bobby-sox idol. I was brought back again after all this to appear with Judy Garland. For the next seven or eight years I almost lived at the Palladium.

Everything seemed to happen at once—I was appearing for a week at the Nottingham Empire with not a worry on my mind other than doing well with the audience. As I entered the stage door, a telegram was thrust into my hand. It said congratulations—I had been chosen to appear before King George the Sixth and the Queen Mum for a Royal Variety Performance. I suddenly began to quake. Although the date was several weeks off I didn't know what they expected of me. I had not had experience of this sort of thing. Let me explain that a Royal Variety Performance then, to what it is now, was quite different. It was not televised, it just came over on radio but millions listened. I believe it had a listening audience of thirty million—when you try to visualise that amount of people, it is practically impossible. There were only a few acts because, naturally, jugglers or acrobatic acts were not for radio. Almost everybody you met heard the broadcast, so it was imperative you did well.

The audiences were the same every year: the first ten rows were filled with people from the film industry who wrote the price of tickets off for tax purposes as donations. The next few rows were agents and friends, and sometimes the public got a few seats. It was very much like an Old Bailey Jury, but with Royalty present. Up and down the sides and across the back in the standing room only area were the press men, looking for a story. That audience had seen everything—it was almost impossible to surprise them. I cannot think of a more frightening audience. As a matter of fact Tommy Trinder, in his warm-up spot before their Majesties arrived, went out and read some press notices about how diabolical the audience had been in previous years. "It's you they're talking about," he cracked—it broke them down a bit but not much. All this I had to face as a comparatively new solo act.

I could hardly sleep at night thinking about it. For me that is something, because I have a reputation for being able to sleep anywhere, even before a big show or any nerve-racking event. I have appeared in sixteen Royal Performances and Galas since then and they haven't worried me all that much. The last one I did, in 1972, I almost missed because I nodded off on the settee at home. But this first one had me like a cat on hot bricks.

A friend, a few weeks before the event, suggested I try confidence pills. They didn't help. I finished up proposing to nine of the Tiller Girls.

At last the big day came, 3 November 1950, twenty-eight years of age, armed with a script that Eric Sykes and I had slaved over for weeks, and all I had was my cheek—I couldn't even get a standing room ticket for Eric. He waited in the pub just round the corner from the stage door.

It might be of interest to have a look at what I had put down in script form for that performance, it may not look much on paper but when it was performed they were still cheering as I made my way to the dressing room, it went as follows:

(Compere's announcement. Max walks on to Music of "Please". Music fades, he speaks)

MAX: Ladies and gentlemen, I wonder if you would be kind enough to help me. It is my job to make you laugh so if I tell a joke that makes you want to smile—will you laugh that little bit more, because, if you don't get good laughs here, the management finds other jobs for you. Here's the first joke. A man walks into a bank, says to the teller: "How much is a pound worth nowadays?" The teller said: "About five shillings." The man puts a pound down and says: "I'll take four."

(As Max notes the reaction to this joke, a stagehand enters and shoves large broom in his hand. Max proceeds to sweep stage)

MAX: (to audience) "Come to the Palladium," they said, "You'll clean up!" (He turns to offstage and continues dialogue): I don't have to do this, I've got money—when I was a kid, I saved sixpence a week—my father made me—every time I put sixpence in my money-box my father used to pat me on the head. By the time I was sixteen, I had twenty-five pounds, ten shillings and a flat head.

(When Max hears this laugh, he turns to offstage again and shouts):

MAX: Listen to that laughter—that deserves more than a broom!

(From the other side of the stage a bucket and mop is thrown on. Max picks up mop and talks to it as Charles Boyer)

MAX: Hedy—Hedy—mon cherie, you are so thin.

(He runs hand up and down mop handle) (This business was cut by the Lord Chamberlain's office)

MAX: I know what I'll do, I'll do my acrobatic act.

(He takes off coat, as he does, two chorus girls enter with small table and two chairs, which they stack on top of table)

MAX: Ladies and gentlemen, I will now do a double somersault, landing on a splits—it is a very difficult trick—just in case of an accident—could I have the applause before I do it?

93

(Audience applauds)

MAX: (Puts coat back on again) Well, I'm not breaking my neck for that! . . .

The act continued on these lines of everything going wrong for the performer. We decided to do "the cup of tea" for a get-off. I was only allowed seven minutes; it went seven at rehearsal—on the night it went nine, but nobody seemed to mind.

The dressing room was full of pressmen and photographers afterwards—the *Sunday Pictorial*, as the *Sunday Mirror* was then, asked to do my life-story—this was written by Peter Noble. The BBC asked me to appear in a new series they were starting with a wooden dummy to be called *Educating Archie*. I signed for three years' pantomimes with Tom Arnold and also a five year recording contract with His Master's Voice label. The first record I made for them was a piece I had written for my act called "Cowpuncher's Cantata"—it was a moderate success on record. I also had the Judy Garland show that was coming to the Palladium which really changed my whole life financially, but first I had to go to the Manchester Palace to appear in *Mother Goose*.

Make no mistake about it, the hardest form of entertainment for a new performer is an English pantomime. These fairy stories have to be acted out with great sincerity. Children have no respect for "names", they want deeds, lose them and they will chatter among themselves, eat sweets or decide to "pay a penny" if you bore them. You are expected to use the stage, not to hold a microphone and give out with a few one-liners. You go into the theatre at approximately one o'clock and it's usually ten-thirty before you leave. Apart from a short break between houses, it is go-go-go. If any young person asks my advice on how to become good at stagecraft I usually tell them to get in a good pantomime.

The difference in my son's attitude after he had done a pantomime season at Southsea a couple of years ago was staggering—before he wanted to be the smarter Sammy Davis Jnr-type of performer. After a season in *Aladdin*, he realised there was a lot more to it. He set about learning it. When I watched him performing after that I was amazed how much he had learned.

One night, whilst I was at the Manchester Palace, there was a burglary. All the dressing rooms had been broken into. Missing from mine was a small radio, some odds and ends and a lighter that was given to me by the teenagers at St Anne's Youth Club in Battersea. I did a bit of charity work for them at various times and to thank me they had a whip-round and bought me this automatic Ronson lighter. It was engraved "To Max from your friends at St Anne's." I was rather upset about the lighter because I knew these kids were not millionaires—the few shillings each they contributed meant more to me than most of my other possessions. I told the police but didn't hold much hope of ever seeing it again.

Several days later, I was making my way to the Commercial Hotel where I was staying and in the half light of the entrance stood a young fellow with his coat collar turned up, all sinister like. He said "Max Bygraves?" I said I was. He held out the lighter. "Recognise this?" I looked. "Yes," I said, "it's my lighter." He told me he had bought it off a fellow who was down on his luck but it was no good to him so if I would like to give him a couple of pounds for it, I could have it.

I have never been one for wallets or pocket-books so I felt in my jacket pocket and handed him two pounds. He gave me the lighter, took the money and was gone. It was pretty obvious he was the one who had broken into the dressing rooms but there was not much I could do about it; besides, I wanted the lighter back.

It wasn't until I got into the light of the reception, I looked at my hand that still held several pound notes but they weren't pound notes. It was "stage money" that I used for a scene in *Mother Goose*. It looked amazingly like a real pound note but on both sides was printed "All that glitters is not gold."

Years later, I did a concert for the inmates of Dartmoor Prison. After the show I was talking to some of the convicts and one reminded me of that night. It was the same fellow. He told the story to all around, including some warders and finished up by saying, "He's a bigger thief than we are—he should be in here." I couldn't convince him that I honestly didn't know it was stage money that I had put in my "going home" jacket.

Maxine, our third child, was born during the run of *Mother Goose*. She was the prettiest of our children—Anthony had looked like a shrivelled up walnut, even the nurses at the hospital had dubbed him "Churchill". Christine I hadn't been able to see because it was hard to get leave in the RAF. I hadn't managed to see her until a few days after she was born. But Maxine was b-e-a-u-t-i-f-u-l. Fair haired, blue eyed and smiling from the time she opened her eyes —a few hours after she was born she was laughing at the world and has been doing so ever since. She works as a florist at present. Her gentleness is a lesson to me. I wish I could get that serenity she seems to capture so easily. She has kept the beauty she had when she entered the world.

When the run in Manchester was over I started a career that took in broadcasting almost every Sunday for the next four or five years. This was on top of my theatre work. It was, I suppose, hard work but I didn't notice any exhaustion. I thrived on it. I was working every day, every night and enjoying every minute.

Educating Archie was a very successful radio show—lots of performers became national names from it: Julie Andrews, Tony Hancock, Robert Moreton, Eric Sykes, myself and quite a few others, not forgetting the brains behind it all, Peter Brough.

Eric Sykes had this quick ear and could tell by any inflection I put into a line how to make it a catch phrase—at one time I had more catch phrases than I could handle. I had the whole country saying things like "I've arrived and to prove it I'm here!" "A good idea—son." "Bighead!" "Dollar lolly." The show won all the awards going, knocking out *Take it from Here* which had become almost a British institution.

The powers that be were ruthless in their handling of the show. Robert Moreton, a very good capable comedian, was dropped after the first year and he couldn't get any work for any other type of show. Then one day we heard the poor man had taken his life by gassing himself. People were "rested" and new voices were put in. Eric Sykes, through not eating, was suffering from malnutrition and was rushed off to hospital. He wrote the scripts from his sick bed.

Julie Andrews was "phased out" of her singing spot when I happened to do a song spot with Archie. Hattie Jaques, Tony Hancock and myself never quite knew as each series ended whether we would be required for the new one. It didn't worry me all that much because I had more work than I could handle but all the others depended on it. It was a lucrative show to be attached to because there were many repeats on English and overseas radio.

Wally Ridley was the man behind Peter Brough. He was and still is the recording manager for the label His Master's Voice. A

The family: Blossom, me, Christine, Anthony and Maxine.

A fishing sketch with Antho

With grandson Michael.

In Sydney, Australia, 1969.

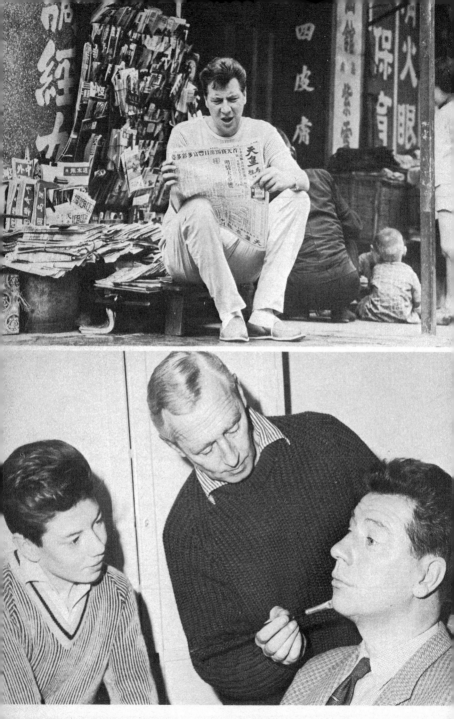

Top: in Hong Kong, reading the daily news!

Bottom: Anthony watches the make-up man go to work.

Top left: from a television show, **Singalongahippie**.

Top right: with pianist Bob Dickson.

Bottom: Dame Edith Evans, who sang for the first time ever on **'MAX'**.

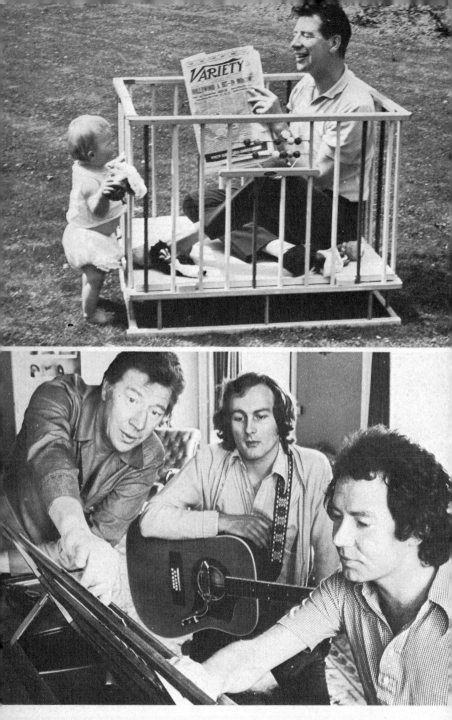

Top: getting a little privacy from grand-daughter Louise.

Bottom: Anthony and David Reilly penning a song for me.

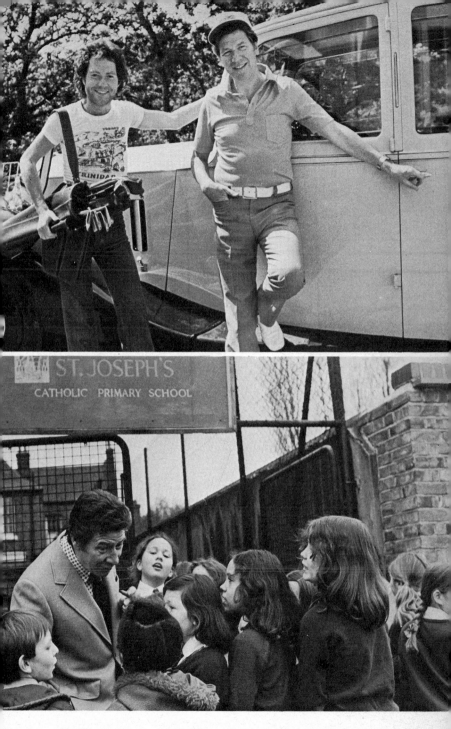

Top: Anthony and me golfing at Bournemouth.

Bottom: back in my childhood days, the school in Paradise Street.

Jock Jacobsen dances with daughter Christine.

short astute man, he was once a song plugger. He invited me to make records with titles like "You're a pink Toothbrush, I'm a blue Toothbrush," also "Gilly—gilly ossenfeffer, Katzenellenbogan-by-the-sea", "I'll take the legs from some old table", "Bighead" and quite a few more. Every one was a winner with the young following we had for *Educating Archie*. Up till then Julie Andrews, who was only fourteen or so, sang in what is known as the "song spot". Gradually her singing spot was dropped and I sang more and more of these funny little melodies, sometimes with Archie, sometimes alone.

I hated this part of the deal. I didn't want to rob a fourteen-year-old girl of her big moment but they assured me that it would all be back to normal the following week, which, of course, it wasn't. I always get a glow when I think of how well Julie did when she left these shores and became a big star because although this talent was right under our noses, few people recognised it. She had to go to America to become a big *name*.

Whilst *Archie* was running, I was asked to appear for a month back at the Palladium with Judy Garland. She was asking such a big salary that quite a few of us on the bill with her had to take a cut. The year before I had been getting £100 a week. They suddenly wanted me to take a cut of £25, making a salary of £75.

Jock argued with Val Parnell. Parnell begged Jock to take it because he knew big things would happen for me by appearing on the same bill as Judy. He was a persuasive man and I appeared with her, taking the cut.

On opening night Judy was all nerves. I had been introduced to her at rehearsal. We had shaken hands and I noticed that even for the rehearsal her hands were wringing wet. The house was packed to see how this legend in her own time was going to turn out without the trickery of filming. She had got quite plump and was more worried about this than how she was going to sing. The band struck up "Somewhere over the Rainbow". The applause was deafening and lasted for a long time; the sort of applause you hear only at symphony concerts. She broke into "The Trolley Song" and finished again to great applause. She was getting great confidence now, each song was going better and better. Now she was singing "Swanee". As she marched off for a "false" exit, her shoe caught the microphone wire and she fell to the ground, she picked herself up, rushed into the wings and cried like a baby. "My first night in England," she screamed, "and I fall on my fan!"

We all stood there in the wings listening to this tumultuous applause. She then became aware of it, wiped the tears from her eyes, straightened her back, walked out on the stage and as an afterthought, took the shoes that had caused the fall off and threw them into the wings. The audience liked that, they went wild, she used that trick at every performance from then on; it was a good piece of stagecraft.

Judy often stood in the wings and watched my act. She had a bell-like laugh and it made me feel good to know she was enjoying what I had to offer.

Something that stays in my memory and has always puzzled me about Judy: one night I was in her dressing room with Charles Henry, who staged most of the Palladium variety shows at that time. She poured herself a drink of gin in a large tumbler. Mr Henry saw this and looked at me as though to say "she's *not* going to drink all that with another performance to do." He quietly took the glass, poured two thirds of it away in the wash-basin—all this he did while she was talking to somebody, he then filled the glass with water from the tap. Then we watched her pick up the watered-down drink and sip it without question.

That year, 1950, I was booked to appear for a summer season at Great Yarmouth. I was sharing the top of the bill with Ronalde the singer and whistler. It was the first time my name had been on the top of the bill. When I got to Great Yarmouth I would walk up and down outside the theatre admiring the billing.

I took Blossom and the three children with me. We rented a house with about eight rooms for £5 a week and enjoyed it tremendously. I still had to go to London at weekends for *Educating Archie*, so I decided to get a bigger car—I was now making £150 a week so treated myself to a secondhand pre-selector Armstrong Siddeley. After the Anglia it seemed like a rocket.

I had also taken a mortgage on a semi-detached house in Friern Barnet, North London. This was our own house and we adored it. What the people who sold it never mentioned to us was that it backed onto a sewerage farm. When the wind was in the wrong direction it smelt awful. I suppose you couldn't blame them not mentioning it—we didn't mention it when we sold it.

Whilst we were away at Yarmouth, the house in London was broken into. The damage was unbelievable. The burglars had thrown the children's toys all around the place. They had opened drink cupboards and drunk themselves into a stupor. A neighbour had seen them entering and they were caught later. It turned out that one of the burglars was a young chap who lived only a few doors away. He got eighteen months.

But now my wife became very jumpy. She had seen the damage and wondered what would happen if I was away on tour and this sort of thing occurred. It made it very hard to leave home for dates up north.

Back at Yarmouth I was enjoying success. One night when I walked off stage I was told there was a telephone call from California, USA. In those days it was like getting a call from the moon. "Who is it?" I asked into the receiver. "It's Judy—Judy Garland—I'm opening at the Palace New York on 16 October. I'd like you to fly over and be on the bill with me." "Me?" I couldn't believe it.

"Yeah you!" She shouted. "Get Jock Jacobsen to call Sid Luft." She gave me a number. Sid Luft was her manager and she later married him. When she'd hung up I phoned Jock in London and told him what had happened.

It was at this time I realised how great a manager Jock Jacobsen is. As I said, I had been getting £150 a week at Yarmouth. The Americans did not know what sort of money the supporting acts at the Palladium got. Jock asked Sid Luft for £3,000 a week, they haggled and settled for £2,500, I would pay all fares and hotel expenses but it left me with a good clear £2,000 a week. I didn't know there was all that money in the world.

The New York opening was even more successful than London. Judy's spot was produced by Charles Walters, a Hollywood director. He brought eight dancing boys from the MGM lot with him. Roger Edens wrote special material for her. I did "We're a couple of swells" as two tramps with her and she tore the place apart. She was the toast of the town.

Every performance was filled with celebrities. I saw Elizabeth Taylor, Montgomery Clift and Frank Sinatra in the front stalls, a few seats back the Gary Coopers, Eddie Cantor and dozens and dozens of others. Judy would work better for another member of the profession than she would for the public. She would send her hairdresser out to the foyer to check who among the famous was in. As the weeks went past and the celebrities had got used up, she got less and less ready to work. In the end the hairdresser, a chap named Ernest Adler, would make up names and swear they were in the audience.

One evening on stage she introduced a very famous name in

America, a columnist named Walter Winchell. He had once been a "hoofer" in Vaudeville. Judy brought him out of the audience onto the stage. They talked about old times and the audience were ecstatic. He did a little "buck and wing"—that's an old fashioned way of dancing—and they loved every moment. He went off to cheers. It made it very hard for Judy to resume her act.

The next night he was in the audience again. It had gone so well the night before that she invited him on the stage again. She couldn't really do anything else as he was the most powerful columnist in America—just a couple of lines in his column was like manna to a performer. This time he stayed a bit longer and went back to his seat to even bigger cheers.

The next night he came yet again, this time he had half a dozen friends with him. Judy invited him up once more and as the spotlight picked him up she noticed he was wearing full stage make-up. He did an even longer spot. It was slowly turning into the Walter Winchell Show.

After this she got wise. She would introduce him as the curtain was coming down and then run for the wings before he could get out of his seat.

Boredom had now set in with Judy. It suddenly became hard work to attend a two-thirty matinee, attend press receptions, do radio interviews, work another show at night. She much preferred the parties and her old show-business friends.

One matinee, I was about to walk on the stage to do my act when the hairdresser came running up to me saying: "Max, can you do a bit longer—stretch it a bit—Judy's not too well." He lifted his elbow in a drinking gesture and threw his eyeballs up to Heaven and was gone. I had an act lasting about fourteen minutes in those days. To pad it out I put in quite a lot of things I had been told to take out when I opened because they reckoned the American public would not understand.

For instance, the darts routine was reckoned to be too English. They said nobody understood the game of darts. I also had a burlesque on Al Jolson, who had recently died. I was warned off this because I was assured he was a legend and should not be burlesqued.

Well, on this particular afternoon, every time I looked into the wings, I could see a stage manager miming the word S-T-R-E-T-C-H! I did everything I had ever done and got results with material that seemed too European for Americans. I was

cheered by the audience, then the curtains came down for inter-
mission.

Judy was still not in a fit condition to appear, so after a lot of
deliberation, it was decided to give the audience their money back
and let them go home. This meant them not seeing Judy Garland.

As I was the only talking act on the bill, they decided I was the
one to go and announce that owing to "indisposition of the star",
all monies would be refunded but, of course, they didn't want their
money back, they wanted to see Judy. I tried to quell them but they
started slow hand-clapping, the same audience that had cheered me
twenty minutes before, were now booing. I had never before been
booed, it was a frightening experience, but it was the first of many
times I had to go out in front of the curtain and make the same
announcement.

As my four-week contract came towards the finish, Sid Luft
asked me if I could extend it for another twelve weeks—it was a
lovely thought to have twelve more weeks at £2,000 plus a week
but I had signed a contract with Tom Arnold to appear in pantomime at Newcastle, this was for only £175 a week. We sent cables
and begged Tom Arnold to let me out of the contract which we
promised to honour the following year but he wouldn't do so—
I was now a hot property in England, so he held me to it. Sid Luft
offered to buy the contract at four times what he was paying me
but it was no dice.

I managed to do five weeks with Judy, then returned to London
with quite a lot of money—even after American tax had been
stopped. I immediately paid up the mortgage I had taken for twenty
years on the house by the sewer and bought a new Jaguar.

I finished the pantomime at Newcastle and then did a new set of
Educating Archie shows. When the new series began we had Tony
Hancock with us. He was most popular and created the catch
phrase "Flippin' kids!"

We did the programme from the Paris Cinema in Lower Regent
Street on a Sunday. We were given an hour for lunch so Eric
Sykes, Tony and myself went to a tiny Greek restaurant called the
Hellenique—it happened to be Tony's birthday so we celebrated
with a bottle of champagne. The manager gave Tony the cork from
the champagne as a souvenir, we were late getting back as we were
all rather "high" from the champers. Peter Brough was very angry
and tore the three of us off a large strip. We all stood looking rather
sheepish because we were in the wrong. We worked hard to please

him but he was in an unforgiving mood right up until show time.

Before the show, we did a warm-up spot, Peter Brough would walk out with Archie, the dummy, then he'd introduce Julie Andrews, Tony Hancock, Hattie Jaques and myself and we'd all do a little "piece" to get the audience in a receptive mood.

To get Peter out of his black mood Tony, who still had the champagne cork, picked up the dummy and placed it by the wire onto the fly of Archie's trousers, expecting Peter to walk in and laugh because it looked most obscene where it was placed, but Brough came into the small room at the side of the stage, picked up the dummy without looking and walked straight on stage. There was no chance to stop him.

He began talking to the audience and suddenly started getting laughs like he had never got before, all the audience had seen the cork but he had not, the most innocuous lines were getting yells of laughter and he was loving it.

When it was time to introduce Tony Hancock, Tony walked straight out and said: "Hello Archie, old son." Then he patted him on the shoulder, and by sleight of hand reached down and removed the cork, even the audience didn't see it go. It wasn't until the following week when Brough was all smiles because the audience ratings were great and he was in a good mood, we told him what had happened. He then laughed as much as we did.

It was about this time I happened to be walking along Charing Cross Road on my way to a music publishing office when I met Bob Dixon. He nodded. I thought I knew him—Bob's like that—he has the sort of face everybody thinks they know. I juggled with him, trying not to ask him where the hell we had met, then I had to. He told me he had been playing piano in the orchestra pit at Yarmouth. He gave me his card and asked me to call him should I ever need a rehearsal pianist. A few days later I needed exactly that. He came to the house at Finchley and has been with me ever since, touring the world several times and never missing a performance except once to travel home because of his father's dying. He has been with me for the past twenty-three years. His favourite joke is "Imagine, if I had been on the other side of Charing Cross Road at that particular time, I'd have still been out of work." He is the most loyal man; when his marriage finished on the rocks, his wife told me that she was leaving him because "he was more in love with Max Bygraves than he was with me".

A few weeks after Bob joined me, I received another call from California to go to Hollywood for another Judy Garland Show. I left in the spring and arrived in Hollywood with my little family, Blossom, Christine now nine, Anthony nearly five, Maxine who was still a baby and Bob Dixon.

Hollywood as a film centre was still the glittering place I had believed it to be. The trams were still running along Hollywood Boulevard into Los Angeles—it cost just ten cents for a seven mile ride. There was Grauman's Chinese Theatre, where all the famous movie stars had put their hands or footprints in cement. Almost the first big star I met when I got there was Clarke Gable.

I had signed up with an American agency known as MCA. Their offices were on Santa Monica Boulevard. They had parking facilities at the rear so I parked the car that I had rented at the back while I kept an appointment with one of the MCA executives.

When I got back to the car there was this handsome man instantly recognisable as Clarke Gable, scratching the back of his head wondering how he was going to back his small MG out of a very small gap.

"Looks like I'm hemmed in," he chuckled.

"It might be easier if I got mine out," I said.

"Okay, you wanna try?"

I couldn't believe that as a kid when I sat at the Storks Cinema in Bermondsey watching him as a pilot, racing driver, muscle man, etc., that the two of us would be standing in a Hollywood car park trying to figure out how to get our cars out.

It was an automatic Chevrolet I had hired. It was important to have the gear in neutral before you started, then lift the gear handle to drive or reverse. I was so excited at all this, I mistakenly put the car into "drive" instead of "reverse" as I shot forward, his bumper scraped the side of my shining, almost new, hired Chevrolet. I heard him say "Jesus Christ!" and turned to find him looking at me like I was a nut. I tried to explain it was my first day in this car. He lifted that one eyebrow and pursed his lips but accepted my explanation.

Luckily, his MG only had a minor scratch. I managed to back out without more trouble.

"You English?" he asked.

"Yes," I stammered.

"You ought to be driving an English car," he yelled as he departed, "like me!" He thought that was a great joke.

I paid a bill of thirty dollars for the scratch on the American Chevrolet.

Another film star who was extremely kind to me during those early days was James Mason. He had seen me appearing in New York and had sent me a letter expressing his admiration. I have the letter to this day.

One evening there was a telephone message to call him at his home. He was married at the time to a vivacious lady, Pamela Kellino. She answered the phone and invited me to their house the following Sunday. I said I wouldn't be able to make it as I had a large family with me and would be entertaining them. She told me to bring all of them so, the following Sunday, we arrived at the Masons' palatial Spanish-style home. It was breathtaking.

Everything had wonderful taste. It was easy even for me "from the buildings" to appreciate the flair and finesse in that room: the furnishings looked like a page from *Vogue* come to life. From the front of the house was a rolling lawn down to a large bathing pool where all the action was.

We were introduced all round and among those I shook hands with was Frank Sinatra. He was having a lean time just then. I found him very sociable and interested in what I was doing. I mentioned that he was responsible for me doing "a cup of tea bit" at the London Palladium. In the middle of me telling him this, Blossom asked me to go to the car and get the baby's bottle, it was time for Maxine's feed and she kicked up merry hell if she didn't get it on time.

As I came through the lounge I saw a beautiful red-headed young woman crying helplessly, her handkerchief up to her eyes. Pamela Kellino was comforting her. As I looked again I could see it was Ava Gardner. I heard that she and Frank had had words but was told not to worry, she would get over it. They were used to their storms.

As we drank Martinis and ate large barbecued steaks, I was talking, with my back to the pool, to James Mason—suddenly his eyes became big and frightened looking. He suddenly dashed forward, fully clothed, and jumped into the pool. I turned to see him removing an inflated rubber ring from around Anthony's legs—he had been slowly drowning and not one of us thirty or more people there had noticed. We laid him on his tummy and pushed out the water he had taken in. An hour later he was alright. From then on, we never took our eyes off them in a pool.

A month later they were all good swimmers: we had seen to it that they learned.

The following evening, Bob, Blossom and I went to the Coconut Grove to see Frank Sinatra who was appearing there in cabaret. The three of us adored his singing, even though in the early fifties he wasn't the name he is today, I often think he was singing better than he did at any other time.

Business was terrible: there were only a few scattered diners; there was no big orchestra, just the resident band, plus Billy Miller his pianist, and Axel Stordahl conducted. A group of people at a table were making a lot of noise so Bob Dixon asked them politely to be a little quieter as he wanted to listen—most of them simmered down but one fellow, a big bluff American football looking type, wanted to pick a fight with Bob, who is only about five feet five. "Look, man," he yelled at Bob, "I'm paying good money to do what *I* want to do." All this was over a plaintive ballad that Sinatra was rendering, "I'll please myself," he clucked. It was impossible to reason with him but he wouldn't give up. Frank went on oblivious to it, although it was almost impossible to ignore him. He suddenly started singing another tune entirely to the one that Sinatra was singing, very loudly.

All through this Sinatra smiled, finished his act, bowed to polite applause and was gone. We finished our drinks and ten minutes or so later, left. On our way out, we saw Frank sitting in a booth with a blond, they were smooching. Bob said "Good thing Ava can't see him." Suddenly, he waved. We walked over to him. As we got nearer we recognised the blond: it was the red-head that had been crying at the Masons' the day before, Ava Gardner. In one day she had changed colour.

We said how sorry we were about "Bigmouth" at the other table. He shrugged it off and said, "It's one of the hazards." He was obviously too happy to care. Last time Frank Sinatra appeared in London, they were asking £100 a seat. Back at the Coconut Grove in 1952 they couldn't fill the place at two dollars a head. When I have had audiences similar to that one at the Grove, and I have, I just think of those words of wisdom: "It's one of the hazards."

During my first week in Hollywood I saw more stars than the astronauts. I met quite a few, too. Sheilah Graham, a well-known columnist for the *Hollywood Reporter* invited me to a luncheon given by the world press for Hollywood movie stars—at this luncheon, she introduced me to Robert Taylor, Joan Crawford, Marlene Dietrich and Arthur Kennedy, all in a few minutes.

The very same evening I went to dinner at Chasens, a popular restaurant with the stars, and was introduced to Jack Benny—he in turn introduced me to George Burns and Gracie Allen, Alfred Hitchcock, Mitzi Gaynor and Franchot Tone. Jack and I got on like a house on fire; we had an approach to humour that could turn us into a couple of giggling children. We remained friends for over twenty years. I went over at different times to appear on his show. He then asked me to go to Las Vegas and do the "interruption" bit he once did with Phil Harris. He flew my entire family, plus Mr and Mrs Jock Jacobsen over to attend the opening.

He was very fond of George Burns, who is a great wit—I brought him over to London to appear on one of my television shows. He was great at rehearsal and had a fund of riveting stories. The one I liked most concerned him and Jack Benny at the restaurant I mentioned earlier, Chasens.

One evening the two of them had finished their meal and were having a coffee when George turned to Jack and said: "How long have we been coming to this restaurant?" Jack thought idly: "Over twenty years—why?" George said: "In all that time the management has never picked up the cheque or paid the bill—we have had dozens of people here—spent thousands of dollars—why don't we shame Dave Chasen into paying our bill!"

David Chasen was the owner and a great restaurateur. "How we gonna do that?" Jack Benny asked.

George said: "When he brings the bill, whoever he gives it to will say: 'If you let him pay that bill, I will never come to this restaurant again.'"

"OK," said Jack, "I've got the idea—we'll argue about it and make him so embarrassed, he'll have to pick the bill up and scrap it otherwise he'll think he will lose two of his best customers."

The bill was brought over personally by Dave Chasen and placed in front of George Burns. George felt for his bill fold to pay, then Jack Benny said: "Dave, if you let George Burns pay that bill, I will never come to your restaurant again—give it to me!"

Dave Chasen picked up the bill and placed it in front of Jack Benny but George Burns just looked at the ceiling and puffed on his cigar. Burns had already tipped off Chasen to bring the bill to him. When Jack realised how he had been caught he laughed for three days.

Jack Benny told me time and time again that he could not ad lib. If he had a script by a writer, he reckoned he was alright. Yet I heard him pull one of the best off-the-cuff lines I have ever heard from a comedian. It was in Las Vegas. We were just leaving the poolside, where we had been sunning ourselves, and a small group of people were waiting for Jack's autograph. Invariably, there is a comedian in the crowd who reckons he is funnier than you, he usually comes up with gems like: "Will you sign this cheque?"

This particular fellow pulled a new one. As Jack was signing the autographs, he piped up quite seriously, "Hey, Mr Benny— do you know who's in hospital?" Jack, quite concerned, said: "No—who?" The witty one said, "Sick people!" The small crowd laughed at this but Jack went on quietly signing his autograph until the right moment, then he turned to the funny man and said, "Not all of them."

It was a sad day for me when I heard the announcer on BBC Radio reporting his death at the age of eighty. I knew him well for the past twenty years and never once did age come between us. We always laughed and thought on the same level. Although he was almost thirty years my senior, his brain had the clarity of a much, much younger man. He was a good man and I feel a lot of affection for the name of Jack Benny.

I finished the engagement which was for six weeks in Hollywood. Judy was the toast of the town, never missing one of the performances. We then moved to San Francisco to appear for six weeks at the Curran Theatre on Geary Street.

Judy got a little bit bored with San Francisco and began missing shows again. I used to dread walking out in front of the house curtain to tell the audiences that "The Management regret owing to circumstances beyond their control . . . etc. etc."

To get the confidence of the audience back, the publicity department asked me to go on some television shows and assure viewers it would be business as usual at the Curran.

I appeared on several afternoon magazine programmes. I was introduced as "The Englishman with the Judy Garland Show." I was not always what was expected because, until the Beatles came on the scene, the average American's idea of an Englishman was either Terry-Thomas or Robert Morley. I think these two characters did more harm for the British than the Boston tea affair. Everybody expected me to turn up in bowler hat, rolled umbrella, sipping tea and saying "Hello, old boy," like the stupid asses Thomas and Morley portray. I have done shows with Perry Como, Bob Crosby, Ed Sullivan and Jackie Gleason and in every one I was asked to play a "pip-pip" Englishman. The only person that didn't ask for this was Jack Benny.

I was telling you about this afternoon programme in San Francisco: this took place from an hotel they named Mark Hopkins. The telecast was from a room at the summit called "The top of the Mark". A woman interviewer, very similar to Joan Bakewell, sort of inquisitor, was asking what I liked and what I disliked about the USA. I talked about the high standard of hygiene in the cafes and snack-bars. We are a lot better in England now but back in 1952 we were very behind at this sort of thing. In America counters were washed and cleaned almost every time a customer leaves. There were clean napkins; the waitresses had clean white uniforms daily; there was a health inspector calling periodically to make sure that this standard was adhered to.

What puzzled me was that in almost every snack-bar, underneath each counter were wads and wads of chewing gum. If you happened to forget, or not know about this, you felt you had to get to a washroom to clean your hands under a tap. It conjured up all sorts of diseases you might get from this.

I mentioned this during the interview—I said I couldn't understand why such a high standard was demanded by the customers and yet they could carry on with this filthy habit.

I collected a fee of twenty-five dollars, which I didn't think was a fortune as I had done several songs, jokes and talked for almost two hours. Nevertheless, I took the cheque and departed. I thought no more about it.

There is a well-known columnist on the West Coast called Herb Caen who writes for the *San Francisco Examiner*. He happened to be watching this particular TV show where I talked about the chewing gum.

Next day, his column was headed: "Limey deplores US gum habit." The piece suggested it was about time Americans got out of this filthy habit of parking gum under counters, tables, seats, etc. I didn't think when I mentioned it on the programme it would snowball like it did, others took it up, radio shows, smaller newspapers and the rival TV companies.

A few evenings later when I made my way to the theatre on Geary Street, waiting at the stage door for me were two executive type fellows: dark blue mohair suits, pale blue shirts, conservative striped ties and the "in" thing then—crew cuts.

They were all smiles, one handed me a card which said they were from a well-known advertising agency. They represented a nationally famed chewing gum. They told me that what I had said on the programme hadn't helped sales too much. I said I was sorry, I hadn't meant to do their clients any harm and they understood. I asked if there was anything I could do. They said there was. I could go on the programme again and make it clear that there is a wrapper, which asks in print to save it, so that when the gum is finished with, it can be wrapped up and disposed of. If I could mention this and read it out, it would put them in good with their accounts.

They told me they could fix it for me to go on the programme, they would pay me two hundred dollars for my trouble, which was a lot better than the twenty-five I had got a few days before. I did it and everybody was happy afterwards. I have often thought since, what would have happened had Jock Jacobsen been there instead of back in London. I can assure you, knowing Jock, it would have cost them a lot more than two hundred bucks.

One Monday morning in San Francisco, I casually opened a newspaper and there in big headlines it said: "Judy marries Sid." On the previous day, the two of them had taken it into their heads to go across the Golden Gate Bridge to be married by a small town Justice of the Peace. When they arrived at the theatre that evening they were like turtle doves.

Thursday came and Sid, who likes the race horses, went off to Los Angeles "on business". When he hadn't returned on the Saturday morning, Judy became quite over-wrought. "I know where the so and so is," she stormed, "He's at the Saratoga race-track—I'll make the so and so come back!" she yelled. "Cancel the matinee!"

Once more I had to go out and tell the audience there would be no show—once more I got booed. Sid was back for the evening show and Judy went on. At the end of the run, I returned to England.

When I got back the first thing I did with, what to me, was untold wealth, was to get my parents a new house. They had always adored Kent. I found them a home not too far from their beloved

London but countrified enough for them to appreciate. The house is in Welling but for the first few weeks I thought I had done it wrong.

My father was still working in the docks so he was able to make the journey quite well by train but he was rapidly coming up for retirement so he was not bothered too much about it—he found a lot of pleasure in the small garden, pottering about. My mother was the main worry—she suddenly had more money to spend than she'd had in her entire life but nowhere to spend it. She knew none of the locals; the street was upper class compared with what she had known in Rotherhithe; even the shops in Welling seemed like Oxford Street to one who had done most of her trading at Mrs Marlow's.

It was then it dawned on me that she *never* complained, not only about Welling but about *anything*. I suddenly realised she had never complained about shortage of money, overcrowding, shortage of food and heat, health, working like a navvy, nothing, she took it all in her stride. The raising of six children who are fine and healthy and as far as I know, today not one of us have had more than a cold or chill, was done without complaint.

But at first she did not like Welling. She missed Rotherhithe too much. She would sneak back on the train to her old pub the "Adam & Eve" and sit there with her friends, then return in the later afternoon having donated quite a bit to the Guinness foundation. How she found her way back is amazing because at times she was staggering.

Then one night, my brother called to say "hello" backstage at the Palladium. Harry looked worn out. He had recently married a pretty brunette named Jean Lewis, who had been chosen as Miss Tate & Lyle, the sugar firm she worked for in East London. Harry had been on night work at the docks and it had taken its toll, he was pale and sick looking, his back had been hurt and he was walking badly. I asked him if he wouldn't be happier in some other business. There and then he made up his mind to leave the docks and learn pub management.

He started with his own pub to manage in Camden Town— suddenly my mother had somewhere else to go other than Rotherhithe. She arrived there from Welling almost daily, helped Jean to look after the new children she had given birth to and sometimes cooked lunches for the customers. She was active and happy.

Nowadays she loves her house at Welling. Almost every week

she travels and stays for a few nights at Norbury. This is where Harry has a thriving business at the Norbury Hotel. He is a popular guv'nor, the father of four wonderful sons, who are a credit to Jean, his wife. I asked my mother if she would like to give up the house and move into a smaller flat that would be easier to manage. "No fear," she said, "it would be like going back to the buildings!"

I did quite a few more shows at the Palladium—at this period, I appeared in *Wonderful Time*, topping the bill with Billy Cotton's Band, the Bernard Brothers and Joy Nicholls.

In one scene, I played a dude known as the Dead Shot Kid—Billy Cotton was the sheriff and Joy Nicholls was Lil the owner of the saloon. In the scene there was a tremble as a cowhand rushes into the saloon to warn everybody that the Dead Shot Kid is on his way. Everybody takes cover except Billy Cotton the sheriff, and Lil. As the Dead Shot Kid I push open the swing doors, grab Lil, give her a big long kiss then turn to the sheriff and say: "Well, don't stand there—introduce us." Bill's next line should have been: "So you're the Dead Shot Kid, huh?" But Bill's way with a line was never very good, unless he was prompted. This night, he sauntered up and said: "So you're the Dead Shit Kod, huh?" The audience laughed for five minutes as his face got redder and redder. The only ad lib I could think of was: "Will you repeat the line, friend." This got another long howl. Bill's answer got even a bigger yock—he said: "No bloody fear."

Obviously, this variation from the script had been reported by Jack Matthews, the stage-manager, a very efficient man. A few days later Bill got a memo from head office, signed by Val Parnell, which said that it had come to Parnell's ears we had used the word "bloody" on the stage, this was not allowed and would we refrain from further deviations of the approved script. Goodness knows what he'd have said if he'd heard about the Dead Shot Kid.

After this I did a season in Blackpool for Tom Arnold in a show called *Latin Quarter*. This was with Winifred Atwell and a new northern comedienne named Hylda Baker. The show broke all records for the sixteen weeks' run.

You have to have your wits about you in this business—during the *Latin Quarter* show we had a walk down finale. All the artistes came forward one by one to take a bow. Winnie Atwell preceded me and as I stood at the back of the staircase ready to walk down, I heard a noise go up like a roar at Wembley Stadium. After a few nights of this, I said to Bob Dixon: "Something happens just before I walk down—it sounds like a big roar that dies as I descend the stairs." Bob walked to the back of the auditorium and heard it too.

We did a little bit of research and found that Lou Levison, who was married to Winnie, had got a "live" microphone from the electrician on the side of the stage and as Winnie walked to the front, he cupped his hands and did a roar that boosted the applause —it was good for Winnie but not a lot of good for me. To fight this, when I got to the front of the stage, I walked along the footlights shouting "More, More". The audience were in that lovely holiday mood to go along with it—it swelled my ovation up to a crescendo. Lou confided to me quietly in the bar one evening that what I was doing in the finale was not gentlemanly, not with another star standing on stage.

I said: "Lou—when you do away with the sound effects over the mike, I will stop saying 'More'." His face was a study because he thought I was unaware of what he was doing.

We have laughed about it since, but, like I said, "You have to have your wits about you."

After the Blackpool season I did some odds and ends and then appeared in the pantomime *Cinderella* back at the Palladium. I topped the bill in this and had some wonderful co-stars: Julie Andrews, Mr Pastry and Jon Pertwee were among an all-star cast. It was whilst rehearsing for this that I had lunch with Billy Cotton. We lunched just off Berkeley Square. Both of us were in a mellow mood as we strolled towards the Palladium, the wine and food had been good. On the way we stopped to admire the Rolls Royces in Jack Barclay's window. In the window was a nearly-new silver grey Silver Dawn. "That's the car you ought to have," said Bill. "How much is it?" I asked. "Let's go and find out," said Bill. The salesman said it would cost £4,500. I didn't have that sort of money at that time: I could have raised about £2,000.

"OK," I said in my half drunken stupor. "I'll give you £2,000 down and ten quid a week." "It's a deal," said the salesman. Not knowing quite what I was doing, I signed the forms.

Two days later it was delivered to my home at Edgware with the number plate MB 1 on it. Bill had gone to a lot of trouble to trace the number from an owner in Cheshire and had it registered in my name as a present. I have had seven Rolls models since then and always kept the MB 1 on them.

Every summer we took the children to Alassio in Italy. We started in 1950 and got to know all the locals. When we started going it was a tiny resort, similar to Worthing; now it is built up and big business, but in the early days the beach was not so crowded and few people knew about it. Sometimes I went on stage at the Cafe Roma and did an act for the English people on holiday and we'd have great fun. The four brothers who owned it are named Berrino. They built the Cafe Roma into a fantastic money spinner, so much so that last year (1974) one of them was kidnapped. The ransom demanded was in the region of a quarter of a million pounds which, as far as I know, they paid. But when we first started going there they were as broke as we were.

Bill Cotton was often on holiday there at the same time as ourselves. During the evening we'd gather in the square and have drinks. On one occasion we learned that on the following day there was to be a local football match—Alassio versus a team from Savonah. We booked seats and, naturally, we were cheering for Alassio. The Savonah supporters didn't like this one bit. As we stood up to cheer the first goal scored by Alassio, one of the away team supporters threw a bottle of Coca-Cola at Billy Cotton. Bill leapt out of his seat and chased him all round the stand but couldn't catch him.

On the side of Bill's face, was a large bump. "Look what he did," he said, showing me the swelling.

"It shouldn't have done that," I said, "it was a soft drink."

From then on I could make Bill fall about laughing by going in a cafe, ordering drinks for the company and a soft drink for him. You can imagine the laughter every time a Coca-Cola was mentioned.

I did another pantomime the following year, back at the Palladium once more. This time the subject was *Mother Goose*, starring myself, Shirley Eaton and Peter Sellers. Somehow Peter couldn't make the character of Mother Goose's husband work. He tried several different make-ups but couldn't get it across. The Goon humour he was hooked on was not broad enough for the vast Palladium stage.

One day, it was at a matinee, to break the boredom he made up as Groucho Marx. In the scene where Mother Goose becomes beautiful, he strutted on, bent in the way Groucho walks, and did a great impression. Ogling Richard Hearne who was playing Mother Goose, he said in Groucho's voice, "I've heard of Lady

Dicker—but this is ri*do*culous!" The band whooped it up; they cried laughing. Peter played it up even more while the rest of the cast looked on waiting for their cue line.

The next day when I walked into Peter's dressing room he was on the verge of tears. I asked him what was wrong and he tossed me a letter that had been delivered by hand from the head office of Moss Empires. It was from Val Parnell. It said in effect that the previous afternoon Parnell had been watching the goings-on from the back of the stalls. What he saw he didn't like one bit. When, and if, he wanted the orchestra entertained he would ask Mr Sellers to do so, until then do the job he was paid for and entertain the public. If he didn't, he would come personally and have him kicked out of the theatre.

By this you can see that even as top artistes we had to toe the line. The discipline was rigid. I think that is why a few of us from the old school have stayed that little bit longer. The art of theatre is seeing it done well; it's as simple as that. By all means make it look unrehearsed but everybody from the electrician down must know the cues backwards then, when the action is demanded, do it with authority. I think Peter would be the first to admit he is a good performer today because he came through that school. There is no short cut. Without an audience you are out of show business. The only way to learn is from those people out there in the dark. They guide you. You can't cheat like you can on radio with dubbed applause or film where an editor can make you great with a look, whilst all the action is being done for you by competent actors. On TV they can make a mediocre joke sound like a great line by boosting the applause. On stage it is purely merit. The only one who can help you is you; if you aren't capable then move over.

After *Mother Goose*, I played the leading part in a film, *Charley Moon*. It was a backstage story with some very good songs written by Leslie Bricusse. "Out of Town" came from it.

The producer was a thorough gentleman named Colin Leslie. It was not a block buster but it did reasonably well—it seems to be liked when it is shown on television now and again.

In 1956 I did yet another long-running show back at Argyll Street. This show was called, *We're having a ball*. It was full of good talent, including the very young and energetic Kaye Sisters, Joan Regan, some great American and Continental speciality acts, plus a young and vivacious chorus—it ran till Christmas and was one of the best and financially most successful revues ever seen at the Palladium.

It was during the run of this show that I was asked to appear in another Royal Variety Show. Some of the names on the bill that year were: Harry Secombe, Laurence Olivier, Dickie Henderson, Bud Flanagan, Ben Lyon, Alfred Marks, Tommy Trinder, Bob Monkhouse, Gracie Fields, Alma Cogan and Liberace.

We rehearsed all day Sunday and up till about 5 pm on the Monday, the show was due to go on at 8 pm. We had just finished rehearsing the finale walk down when a voice from the stalls asked for "Quiet!"

On to the stage walked Val Parnell and very quietly said: "Ladies and gentlemen, I am very sorry to have to tell you that the performance is cancelled." He went on to explain that the Suez Crisis was very serious. Anthony Eden was going to speak to the nation after the six o'clock news. Her Majesty did not think it was her place to be at a theatre during a world crisis and had reluctantly sent the message from Buckingham Palace that she would not be attending.

We were all stunned. For most people it was the event of a lifetime but the one it hit most was Liberace. When I got to the dressing room, he was crying, his shoulders were shaking with emotion.

It wasn't hard to understand either. We give our services free to help actors and actresses who have not had it so good—all proceeds go to these people who are now in retirement and have been unable to get insurance or superannuation schemes as people with ordinary jobs can.

It had taken Liberace a long time to get to England, as he had his dear old "mom" with him. She had a phobia about flying so, by the time he had come overland to New York, then by boat across the Atlantic, most of it at his own expense, it was enough to make most people want to cry.

We all stood around in the number one dressing room, which had turned into a conference room—there was me, Jimmy Wheeler, a red-nosed comedian, Winifred Atwell, who was there visiting Liberace and Tommy Trinder, Bob Monkhouse and Dickie Henderson.

Somebody poured a drink and we drank. Jimmy Wheeler got through about five drinks while we were on our first. As he drank his fifth he suddenly opened his violin case, took out his false moustache, stuck it under his nose, raised the bow to the violin and said to the assembled company: "Ladies and gentlemen—I've been rehearsing this bloody act for a fortnight, so somebody's going to hear it!"

He then went into this routine he had rehearsed for Her Majesty. As he got deeper and deeper into the act he let a few choice words go—to visualise that act being done in front of the Royal Box was hilarious.

What a few moments before had seemed like a wake, suddenly turned into hilarity, Liberace dried his tears and began to laugh. Just as suddenly cars were organised and we all drove back to Winifred Atwell's house in North London—food and drink were organised. All I can remember of the whole affair was leaving Winnie's house at about 4 am seeing her and Liberace seated at a grand piano playing "Chopsticks".

I was now making a lot of money. Jock had done some good deals for me. I was topping bills at all the major theatres. He had booked me in on percentage terms. That way we supplied the supporting bill, plus the star, which was me, the theatre provided the band and stage staff and we usually got sixty-five or seventy per cent of the takings.

Of course, as my salary got higher, Jock's percentage got higher. He was having it good too, because invariably the supporting acts paid a commission to him.

Jock kept urging me to invest—he reckoned the best investment was gold—buy gold and put it away, watch the price grow, he said.

I took his advice and went to Garrards in Regent Street—I selected an eighteen carat solid gold cigarette case and paid £175 for it, a lot of money in those days.

To make use of it, I bought cigarettes to fill it. I hardly smoked in those days. The case seemed to weigh me down—I was rather sorry I had bought it after a few days. It put my suits out of shape and I was always worried about leaving it around in dressing rooms in case somebody a bit light-fingered had it away.

Eventually, I put it in the bank vault and forgot about it. It must have been twenty years later, I thought I'd better trade it in. I didn't smoke any more, there was little use for it so I took it back to Garrards—this was my investment in gold.

I was given £175 for it—the same amount I had paid twenty years before. If I had put that same £175 in some good stock, it would have been worth a good £1,000 today. I'm sure it would. So much for gold investment.

We were having a lot of fun playing the stock market too. Eric Sykes and I became avid readers of the *Financial Times*. We would call the brokers and buy two hundred pounds of this stock, two hundred pounds of that. We got very excited—as one price rose, we invariably had another share go down, so really and truly, when we cashed in our chips, we hadn't really done all that well— the ones who seemed to be doing the best were the brokers—they got you coming and going, a fee for selling and a fee for buying.

These brokers came up with tips to buy and we would buy. I never had one tip that ever paid a dividend of any dimension; any bank deposit account would have paid better than most of the shares I held for several years. I came to the conclusion that stock-brokers knew very little about share buying, or if they did, they were not going to tell punters like Eric and me.

Share buying became our biggest past-time, we bought books on it; we had the *Investor* delivered weekly. I bought a book by an ex-Vaudeville dancer called: *How I made one million dollars on the Stock Exchange*. Eric and I phoned each other several times a day; the talk in our house was like Throgmorton Street.

One day Blossom said to me, "Look at this wonderful invention I've just purchased." She showed me what looked like a miniature vacuum cleaner. It was a thing for shampooing carpets. The idea was to fill it with carpet shampoo and run it across the carpet. We had been paying bills of fifteen pounds or more to have the carpets shampooed. With this gadget and a little elbow grease she said she could do it for twenty-five shillings. She demonstrated it and it worked exceedingly well.

"Good girl, Bloss," I said. "Nice to know you're saving money."

"You ought to find out who are making these," said Bloss, "they are going to clean up."

"Now, now, darling—I'm the comedian."

"You ought to buy shares in them, Max—this is a great thing for housewives."

I kept stalling every time she suggested that I buy some of the shares. I didn't want to buy shares in a gimmick like that, I wanted to dabble in the giants like ICI or Marks & Spencer. The makers of this thing was a firm called British Xylonite—big deal! I'd never heard of them.

One morning, I was talking to the broker on the phone, Blossom kept prodding me and saying: "British Xylonite!—British Xylonite!" I hung up and said to her: "Look, if I give you a thousand pounds—will you do your own investing?"

"Yes—I will!"

"Right—here's a cheque for £1,000—it's a present—put it on a horse—buy shares—do what you like with it—but let me do my own share buying."

She took the cheque unbelievingly. "Can I really do what I like with it?" she asked, eyes all wide.

"Anything you like." With that I left to go to the matinee at the Palladium.

The following morning, I had just woken from a deep sleep. Bloss always got up early to see the kids off to school.

As I focused, I saw her standing at the side of the bed with her forefinger in her mouth, rather like a little girl who has done something wrong. She was holding a letter.

"I think you're going to be angry," she said.

"Why?"

"Look," she handed me the letter. It was a note from my stockbrokers for £5,400.

"Christ—what do I owe that for?"

"British Xylonite," she said.

She told me the full story. When I had left for the theatre, she had phoned the stockbrokers, who she knew fairly well, and asked to buy some British Xylonite shares. She had this amazing faith in the carpet shampooer. The broker had asked her how many she wanted and she said, "A thousand," meaning a thousand pounds' worth. He had bought a thousand shares. The market price was a few pence over £5 each, hence the bill for £5,400—I had never invested more than a couple of hundred pounds in shares—I wasn't even sure I had that amount. I grabbed the phone and dialled the brokers.

"Do you want us to sell? You'll lose a lot in stamp duty and commission," they said.

I didn't want to be in for about £500 loss, so I asked the broker to watch them and if they went too low to sell. But they didn't go low, they began to *climb*. At first, just a few pence, then a few shillings, then one for one shares, then woof! Along came the Distillers group and made a takeover.

When Blossom traded them in several weeks later, she made over £5,000 and in those days there was no Capital Gains Tax.

It taught me a great lesson. Quietly, without telling her, I sold all the rubbish I had bought from spending hours over a pink *Financial Times*. I don't think I ever bought another share from that day. Yes, I did, I bought one lot more.

I was invited by John Bloom, the washing machine tycoon, to spend a weekend aboard his yacht in the south of France. It was the weekend of the Monte Carlo Grand Prix. John's chauffeur picked Blossom and me up at Nice airport and took us out to this magnificent yacht standing in Monaco harbour.

Blossom was very impressed by it all. The boat had a lift, a piano, an aquarium, beautiful suites to dine in, to sleep in—it had everything.

We were made very welcome with drinks, etc. All through dinner and drinks John was being continually called to the phone. I would hear him murmur: "Alright, buy thirty thousand." It was an experience to see this whiz kid in action. He wasn't still for a minute. Ann, his wife, was the perfect hostess and made us more than comfortable.

We parted, because I had to be at work on the Monday. On the flight back I kept marvelling how such a young man could run such a vast empire as he was doing and come from the same humble background as myself.

A few days later I received a call from Andy Neatrour, an acquaintance I knew from show business. Andy did a public relations job for John Bloom. Andy has recently been awarded the OBE and is a most honourable man.

"Hi, Max," he said. "John (meaning John Bloom) has a company called English and Overseas with some shares to sell—but he only wants a few of his friends to have them, people like Jack Hylton, Bernard Delfont and yourself—they could go down, of course, but we expect them to go up."

"Thanks, Andy," I said, "I'll have one thousand pounds' worth."

A little while after I bought, John Bloom went bankrupt. I lost the thousand pounds and Blossom said: "You should have bought British Xylonite!"

One night after a show at the Palladium I put the key in the front door to find my wife standing there white faced and anxious. "Have you seen Anthony? He hasn't arrived home from school." Most nights he was in bed at 8.30 pm. Where could a twelve-year-old be at this time? "He is probably at his friend's house," I said. "He'll be home soon."

I had some supper. It was getting towards midnight.

"I'll have a walk round the streets. He is probably having a chat on the corner and unaware of the time."

I put my coat on and went out. Sometimes I thought I saw his tiny figure, but it was only the shadows playing tricks. I looked at my watch. Midnight.

I turned towards home, thinking . . . "By now he'll be home and in bed, and that will be good because I won't have to chastise him too heavily."

I opened the door but my wife's face told me he had not arrived.

I knew he was fascinated by London, only twelve miles away. I got into my car and drove slowly along the main road, hoping to see him. There was no sign of a young boy in short trousers, with unruly hair and a freckled face.

It was almost two o'clock when I got back. My wife, by now red-eyed with crying, opened the door. We now had the same thoughts . . . what if anything had happened to him?

I went to the police station. All was quiet. No accidents had been reported.

I asked the desk sergeant to phone if any news came through.

I took another slow drive through the streets. I knocked at his various friends' houses. Sleepy-eyed parents came to the door and assured me that their sons were fast asleep in bed.

My wife and I watched the dawn rise. The phone rang with a suddenness that made us jump.

It was the desk sergeant. "Is he home yet, sir?" I told him he was not. "Alright, I'll put an alert out."

The noise of the phone had wakened my two daughters. They sensed something was wrong when they saw us fully dressed at that hour.

We quizzed them on whether Anthony had intended going some place unusual. Had he any new friends?

I went to the school and asked the head master if any of the boys might know anything about Anthony. They called an assembly, but not one of the two hundred boys could help.

Somehow the press got the story, the police began to get phone calls of a young boy seen alone in places as far apart as Southend, Guildford and Brighton. Cranks phoned in the most terrible stories. My wife was a complete wreck. I wanted to cry. I said a silent prayer . . . "Please, God, keep him safe. Don't let anything happen to him."

And then the tears came. I couldn't hold them back. My body shook. When I had cried enough I tried to dry my eyes to show the family that we had to keep our heads.

Anthony walked into the house that evening about six o'clock —as if he had only been out for half an hour.

He told us he had decided to go to see his aunt in Sussex. It had got late and she told him to stay.

His mother cuddled him, both his sisters cuddled him and I kicked him up the arse.

During the run of *We're Having a Ball*, I wrote a song called "You Need Hands"; it was a success and from it I won the Ivor Novello Award as Songwriter of the Year. It was in the top twenty for about sixteen weeks.

To follow up this success, I wrote another song entitled "You Gotta Have Rain". This won me the ITV Songwriter of the Year Award and it looked like I was set on a good sideline as songwriter but at that particular time rock and roll was taking over.

All that was needed were a few banal lyrics done to a rock beat —the more repetitious the more chance of a hit. There was no way I knew how to write this sort of material and slowly I gave up the idea of trying to write commercial songs. All I concentrated on was writing material for my own act.

Slowly the music halls closed down—skiffle and rock were the only accepted forms of entertainment. Up came names like Tommy Steele, Marty Wilde, Billy Fury, Cliff Richard, Wee Willie Harris and a host of others. These youngsters were the rage, they performed in town halls, concert halls, large pubs, they didn't need the music halls. Suddenly it was records; from records on to television in shows like *Six-Five Special*; from there on the road, where teenagers screamed and thronged to get a look at their idols. What they were singing didn't matter, it was hysterical participation from the audience that mattered—if you were able to generate that sort of abandon from the kids, you were in business.

People like myself, Frankie Howerd, Frankie Vaughan, David Whitfield and established comics, were relegated to "also rans"— overnight, we became the "old school". It seemed if you were not on television, you were out of business. It mattered not that you were doing well in some other engagement, you had to be seen on the box.

In the middle of all this I was offered a film. It was quite a dramatic story—it concerned a family of East End children whose father had murdered their mother, he was sentenced to death and the children were put into an orphanage. I played the part of an electrician doing some electrical work at the orphanage and during my time there got tangled up in the children's story.

The movie was called *A Cry from the Streets*. It won awards at the Edinburgh Film Festival. It was the only British film selected for the Moscow Film Gala and won the New York Critics Award for the best film of the year.

My leading lady was Barbara Murray, who has proved Lewis Gilbert's faith in her by the great performances she has given in television series over the past six or seven years.

Lewis Gilbert directed the picture and of the few pictures I have made with different directors, I found him the most sensitive. I honestly believe that could I have had his direction for a few more movies, I could have been a good screen actor. He was the only director that would come up to me before a take and say things like: "In this next scene you are bloody well annoyed—you feel like telling the matron to get stuffed—but with the kids looking on you daren't, so you bottle it up and just nod 'Yes'."

These sort of instructions I found easy to follow—when the film was assembled, I found I had got it all together. On other pictures I had made, I got little or no guidance. I overplayed and was far too big in my animation. Once an action is on a cinema screen measuring thirty by twenty feet it becomes exaggerated, but Lewis controlled all that.

When we were in the early days of the film he asked me to come with him to the King's Cross district to find fifty or sixty kids to play the part of orphans. We arrived at some buildings very similar to the ones I had been brought up in.

We got out of the car and wandered towards a group of kids who were playing with a tin can as a football. They were scruffy and just what we needed. In no time the mothers of these children were around us having recognised me from the TV. We asked one of the mothers if she could organise about fifty children for the following day—this she said she would do for four o'clock the following afternoon.

The next day, Lewis and I arrived at the same spot and there ready for us were fifty children but not a bit like we wanted them, they all had their best suits on, hair slicked down with Brylcreem, some of them had little bow ties on—it was obvious they had had pep talks from their parents to be on their best behaviour.

I talked to some likely ones—David Bushell was a five-year-old, front teeth missing, mischievous and oblivious to the world, he was just right for filming. When I tried to see how he spoke, I said: "What does your daddy do?" Without an eye flicker, he replied: "Kicks me up the arse."

At the premiere, I told this story to the film censor, Mr Trevallyn. He told me that had we left it in the film, he wouldn't have cut it, but this was pre-permissive days and Lewis felt sure it would have finished up on the cutting room floor.

We booked all these children for the film for several weeks. David Bushell was the biggest bag of mischief, he was almost uncontrollable.

The shooting of a film is puzzling to a lot of people—for economics, it is not filmed in sequence: sometimes a scene can be done but the follow-up could be filmed several weeks later, although it could be just a few seconds after when it is laced together. Therefore, it is most important that one continues to look the same throughout the entire shooting period. The continuity lady is paid good salary to ensure that everything looks the same from one scene to the next.

With three quarters of the film shot, David goes home to King's Cross one evening and returns the next morning almost bald. He had taken into his head to cut all his hair off with his mother's kitchen scissors. Now, the make-up department had to make him a wig to match the previous shots he had been in. This they had to fix with hair clips and toupe tape.

The cameras would roll for a "take", everything was going fine, then all of a sudden his little fingers would push their way under the wig and David would begin to scratch his head. The director would shout "Cut" and they'd try again. This time he'd rip the whole wig off and throw it at the cameraman. There was hardly a person on the studio floor that could stifle the laughs after "quiet" had been called. At one time the film was right on schedule. After David's sojourn in Vidal Sassoon-land we were three days over.

In the end we had to re-shoot an earlier scene, alter the dialogue to his big sister saying to him: "Come here, I'm going to cut your hair, it's too long." Then she picks up the scissors, puts a towel round his neck and then as she begins to cut at the wig, they dissolve to the next scene.

Another reminder of *Cry from the Streets* is a young lad. I won't tell you his real name because today we are friends. I admire him tremendously and I think he has the same feelings about me.

I'll just call him Mickey. He was coming up for school leaving age. He was a bright-eyed, toothy, perky young man who looked very much like a young Tommy Steele. He had had a tough childhood. His father had left home when he was small, his mother went out to work and most of the time he roamed the streets of the King's Cross area.

We became friends during the shooting of the film and I told him when we finished that should I ever be able to help him, let me know. As soon as he left school a few months later, he came to me and asked for a job. At the time we needed a receptionist at my office in Leicester Square. I suggested to Jock Jacobsen that Mickey might do. We took him on and in one hour he had mastered the switchboard—most girls took a week to learn the workings—he answered the phone politely, took messages, asked callers to wait, he made tea, ran errands and we liked him, he got on well with this great personality he has.

One Monday, I walked into the office and saw him trying to hide his face from me. I walked him over to the light and saw that he didn't have a square inch of skin that hadn't been scratched, the scratches had festered and he looked the mess I had looked all those years before when I came through barbed wire. "What happened?" I asked him. He told me he had been playing football in the park the day before, which was a Sunday, and as he ran after the ball, he had been unable to stop himself, he had run smack into some barbed wire.

I said he had better get it seen to and walked into my office. I stopped for a moment to think about those terrible scratches and something didn't ring true. It seemed most unlikely that any parkkeeper would put barbed wire up near a football pitch for kids to run into.

I felt he was concealing something; I buzzed for him. He walked into my office like a hang dog. "Mickey," I said, "I want you to tell me the truth—who did that to your face?" He began to cry. "My mother," he sobbed.

"Your mother?" I couldn't believe it. I took him with me to the RSPCC office which is quite near my offices. The cruelty to children officer was appalled at what he saw and made investigations. The day before it seemed that Mickey's mother had been in the pub until two o'clock. He was playing football at 2.30 pm and wanted his dinner first. She was a long time getting it. They had words. Mickey threw his dinner at her. She flew at him in a rage and clawed him.

The officer found out that they were both as much to blame. They were both now very sorry and promised it would not happen again.

Several weeks later, Mickey left our office to work at Smithfield Market for treble the money we were able to pay him.

After a few months, a probation officer came to see me. Mickey had been caught thieving and had given my name as a reference. I talked for a long time with the probation officer and Mickey was put on a year's probation.

I had completely forgotten about him when a letter from the Sheriff of Nottingham arrived. Mickey had been caught hijacking a lorry with two million cigarettes from a cafe on the A1 road. Once again, he had given me as a reference. I wrote a long letter to the court about Mickey's background and asked them to give him one more chance.

His accomplices were sent away for three years but Mickey was given two more years' probation. I also wrote to him a stiff letter and told him it was the last time I was going to try to protect him, so he had better pull his socks up.

I didn't hear any more from him until two years ago. He came to see me at the Victoria Palace to ask if I could come and do a concert for some poor children at King's Cross. He told me he was now married and going straight. He was advertising manager for a popular London entertainment magazine and enjoying life. He was also helping children who weren't as fortunate as he was, hence the call. I went and entertained the kids at King's Cross for an hour or so and Mickey was very proud, but not as proud as I was of him. He even gave me a generous write-up in his magazine.

I thought it was time to do some television. I had been doing a few odd guest shots and record programmes but never a series.

In 1961 I got an idea for an outdoor comedy show. Nearly every show was a studio show in those days. I thought it might be nice to have a different location and suggested Alassio in Italy.

ITV liked the idea and I helped to pioneer this type of comedy.

I got Eric Sykes and Peter Dulay to help me with the scripts. With Dicky Leeman as director and a team of technicians, we left for Alassio to shoot six half hours in three weeks. The show was called *Roamin' Holiday*. I discovered a little Italian girl named Piccola Pupa and used her in the shows as a guide and interpreter. It was a winner as a show—ATV repeated it three times and then sold it to countries all round the world. Before we took the film crew to Alassio, the average number of holidaymakers there was about half a million. The following year, two million people vacationed there. I was made honorary mayor of the town.

By now Christine was eighteen, she had fallen in love with a young, handsome floor manager with the film crew, named Michael Richards. When we returned to London, they courted. A year later they were married at the little Catholic church in Edgware. It was a wedding with lots of my show business friends there. I had just bought a restaurant with Leslie Bricusse in Stanmore and we held the reception there.

Mike and Christine found a nice little house in Barnet, not too far from the ATV studios at Bushey where he worked.

A few months later Christine told Blossom and me she was going to make us grandparents: we were both thirty-nine. On hearing the news we both got dressed-up, drove into London, had dinner at the Berkeley Hotel, then finished up "twisting" until four am as our celebration.

We had decided that with Christine married, we could do with a smaller place to live. I found a plot of ground out in Surrey, near Oxshott, and decided to build one that would give us all we required in a house.

My wife spent months planning it with the architects. When it was ready we got a landscape gardener to plan the three acres of meadow I had purchased. When it was finished, it was a dream. *Country Life* devoted four pages to it and various magazines were always phoning to see if they could come and take pictures. This was a great source of annoyance to Blossom. She is very individual, her taste is impeccable and almost every time after the pictures appeared, she would see her ideas in some other periodical.

The house had five bedrooms and five bathrooms en-suite, it was Scandinavian-style with billiard room, large lounges, enormous kitchen, staff quarters and glass, lots of glass to brighten up the place. The garden backed on to the second fairway of the Leatherhead Golf Club, which made it almost possible for me to fall out of bed into a bunker.

At this time, Eric Sykes and I had taken up golf. I was doing very well in my profession. I had films on offer: I could work almost anywhere; managements wanted me for summer shows; I'd had quite a few hit records. I was on radio and TV regularly. It was almost impossible to be in Britain and not know the name of Max Bygraves, or so I thought.

What made me change my mind about my name being on everybody's tongue was during a game of golf Eric Sykes and I played at St George's Hill Golf Club. We were both twenty-four handicap players in those days. Eric had bought this house on the St George's Hill Estate, which also backed on to the golf course. He had made an application to become a member of St George's but had heard nothing.

On this particular day we were ambling, trying to get our ball from the tee to the hole in less than nine or ten strokes, when two balls landed on the fairway almost hitting us. We looked up to see two irate red-faced gentlemen strutting down towards us, walk up to their ball and hit their second shots; nobody said a word. We let them get ahead and two more balls came down.

We had obviously gone off the first tee as some sort of competition was starting, but we had seen no warning of this anywhere on the tee and the steward had said nothing when we paid our fees.

Next day Eric received a letter from the secretary of the club, who wrote:

Mr Sykes,
    You were on the course yesterday during a club competition. You did not bother to call any of the players through.
    I understand that you are desirous of becoming a member of the club, if this is the sort of behaviour we can expect I urge you now to forget it. This also applies to your friend Max Hargreaves.
                                                        Yours truly,

From that day, Eric has often called me on the phone, when I have picked up the receiver, he says, "Can I speak to Max Hargreaves."

The golf club incident happened fifteen or sixteen years ago. Eric still lives there and still is not a member.

*　　　*　　　*

The house at Oxshott was heaven. There was lots to do: grass to be cut, fences to make, rooms to design. I hoped that one day when I was through, I could retire there. I loved to open the big doors wide during the summer and listen to the dozens of different birds giving out with their songs; they came right up to the doors for feeding. Or, if I felt like it, I could put a few clubs in a bag and saunter up the fairway, hitting a few balls. Blossom loved it; it was heaven.

One Sunday morning about seven am I was woken up by the phone ringing. I put the receiver to my ear: "Hello." A timid voice said: "Daddy?" Half awake, I said: "Yes, who is it?"

"It's Christine."

"Hello, darling, what are you calling at this time for?"

"Michael has had an accident."

"Oh—is he hurt?"

"I think he's dead."

"He's what?"

"He's dead."

"Where are you?"

She told me she was at their house with her few-months-old baby, Louise. I told her to wait and I'd get there as soon as I could.

I dressed quickly, so did Blossom. I told her that Mike had had an accident and I was going to Christine's; she insisted on coming.

I broke every traffic rule in the book to cover the twenty miles on that Sunday morning—I made it in half an hour.

When I got there her eyes were red as she sat listless in a chair unable to believe what she had been told.

Michael had been working late at the studio. A friend whose car wouldn't start asked Mike for a lift. Mike drove him all the way home. It was to a district he didn't know too well and, while taking a bend, he had skidded into a tree.

We had up till then never had a death in the family. I didn't quite know how to handle it. I only know that looking at my daughter sitting there so helpless, I'd have given anything—fame, fortune, my life, could he have been brought back.

Mike was buried at the small cemetery in Barnet. Christine and my granddaughter came back to live with us again. At nineteen, she had been married, a mother and widowed. To make life harder, she found she was a few weeks pregnant with a second child.

There was George, Paul and Ringo
They were shouting out "Bingo!"
Back in those good old days.

Your car, you could park it
You could play the Stock Market
They were the good old days.

We would dance at the Ritz
To those Lionel Bart hits
We drank champagne with our lobster mayonnaise.

England was swinging
Hippy bells were a-ringing
Back in those good old days.

It seemed that Christine was never going to get over the death of her husband. Michael John, her second baby, had not been an easy birth and her health had suffered.

In the midst of all this, I had been offered a twelve-week engagement in Australia. I had just finished a show that had been imported from the USA called *Do-re-mi*. It was a musical and not really a good choice. When you are on a small island like ours, it is hard to hide; it is different for American entertainers: New York is three thousand miles from Los Angeles and there are all the capital cities well spaced. In England, places like Wolverhampton and Birmingham are only a bike ride away; same if you go to Leeds and Bradford.

I had already done fourteen shows at the London Palladium—my name was constantly up on the billboards, now with *Do-re-mi* I was at the Prince of Wales Theatre, just off Piccadilly Circus. We ran for eight months. It was a hard show, I was hardly ever off the stage and when we walked on for the finale, the audience would ask me to sing "You Need Hands," or "Tulips from Amsterdam". It all seemed so in vain.

I vowed I would never take any notice of critics again after that show. I got great reviews from most of them, they called me gallant for breaking new ground, they said I had a comedy genius that hadn't been evident before. They also said that I had a singing voice that was a revelation—one critic compared me with Lanza. It was nice to read these critiques but the customers didn't come. We managed to survive and came out even. This I was thankful for, because I have boasted that throughout my time as a top of the bill I have never lost money for a management. I am expensive but everybody has made money on every bill I have topped. I vowed I would back my own expertise against the critics in future.

When the offer for Australia came in 1965 I took it for several reasons. First, I thought it would be a good idea to show the kids the world. Secondly, it would rest me from the London scene and, thirdly, I could take Christine with me, away from all the memories that seemed so close at hand.

Even though Mike's death was now ten months away, she had got no better; she had no interest in anything, not even her new son.

Anthony had done several "bits" with me in shows so I taught him a routine which we worked on and made into a very funny piece of business for the Australian tour.

Christine was coming as my secretary. Blossom was going to look after us all. Maxine I hoped was going to continue her studies as a student. We also took Kathleen, a lovely Irish girl from Belfast to act as nanny to the children, Louise who was about sixteen months and Michael John, who was just a few months.

So one early morning in March our contingent left London Airport for Melbourne: Blossom, myself, Christine, Anthony and Maxine, plus Louise, Michael John, Kathleen the nanny, and Bob Dixon.

I felt like the tour operator every time we landed. I would be checking baggage, bodies and hand grips. I was up and down like a yo-yo, getting the children drinks. In places like Karachi, Calcutta and Singapore, it was hard to stop the children from having cold drinks, yet we didn't want them drinking out of those bottles and glasses because in those days, these places were not noted for their hygienic standards.

It was pre-jet age: the journey took us about thirty-eight hours to get to Sydney where we had to leave the BOAC plane and board an internal flight to Melbourne. This meant a wait of two hours in the transit lounge.

When it was time to board the plane for Melbourne, I did my checking all again—making sure we were "all correct". We left the lounge to board the plane. We were all fatigued and longing to have baths and get to bed. As we got ready to fasten our seat belts, I saw Kathleen look round the seats and then put her hand up to her mouth in fright, she dashed forward and out of the plane just as they were about to take the boarding steps away. She had left the baby, Michael John, in the lounge.

The aircraft suddenly became active, with shouts to the pilot not to start the engines. Blossom rushed up to the flight deck; Anthony was laughing his head off, Maxine was crying. I was trying to keep everybody normal. A few minutes later I looked out of the window and saw Kathleen hurrying towards the plane pushing the stroller with Michael John strapped in and a couple of officials trying to

Blossom gets a kiss for enduring thirty years of marriage.

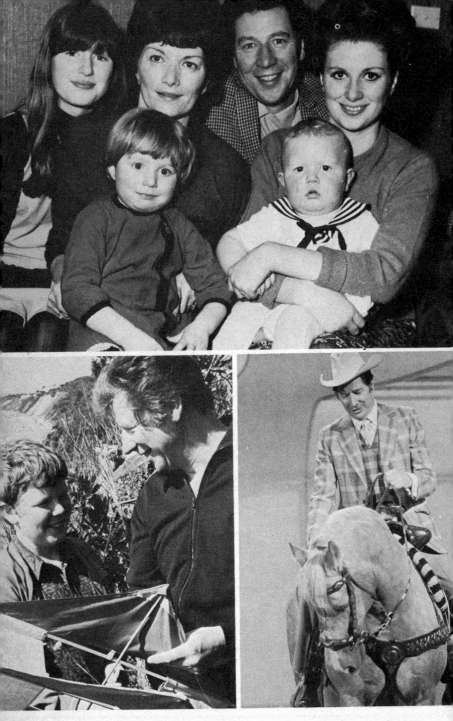

Top: the family is growing; Anthony had left for Hong Kong.
Bottom left: Max with grandson Michael—
and the kite that almost cost me my life!
Bottom right: with Goldie on the stage of the London Palladium.

Me—hanging on to the clothes line I went down the cliff with!

Top: the family in Honolulu—Max, Blossom, Christine, Michael, Anthony, Maxine and Louise (1966).

Bottom left: Max with some of the gold discs for his Singalong albums.

Bottom right: with buddy and fellow golfer, Eric Sykes.

Top: taking the entire staff to Brighton for the day (1973).

Bottom: back in my young man's days—a scene from **Swingalongamax**(

Variety Club Award—Show Business Personality of 1973.

Ah!

Inset: the house at Bournemouth (1975).

keep up with her. She was crying. We grabbed her and the pram into the plane, they locked the doors, the engines roared and we were on our way to Melbourne. From that day, Kathleen carried him in a sling on her back, Indian fashion, especially at airports.

The show was a big success in Melbourne where we stayed for six weeks. We all lived at the Southern Cross Hotel and although I was being paid a lot of money, my expenses were crippling, especially as I had to pay lots of other fares from England and all round Australia. I had to hire two cars, one Christine drove and one me, plus a fantastic hotel bill. I liked the Australians, many of them were uncouth but if you went along with it they were OK. One fellow who had seen the show walked up to me in the bar at the Southern Cross and stuck his hand out to shake. He said in a loud Aussie drawl—"Congratulations, matey—I saw your show the other night—I usually hate the f-----g sight of Pommies but you grew on me!" Then he shook my hand like a pump handle while he stood me at least six cans of Fosters. I left the bar reeling, my family had never seen me drunk before: they all thought it was great fun.

I have never been a drinker. I can only remember being drunk twice or maybe three times in my life but that Aussie beer seemed too potent to me. Bob Dixon thrived on it; he put an extra stone on which he has never lost since.

One incident will stay in my memory for ever. Christine decided to go out to a party for the first time since her husband had been killed. The film *Tom Jones* was showing in Melbourne so a big party was organised a little way out of the town. It was fancy dress: guests were asked to dress like the characters in the film. The men wore wigs, three cornered hats, silver buckled shoes, etc., while the ladies dressed mostly in laced caps, long dresses with plenty of bosom showing. It was a great success.

We, Blossom and I, shared a suite with Christine at the hotel and on previous nights I had heard sobbing from the room she slept in. It was obvious she was having thoughts or dreams of Mike.

On the night of the party, I heard the door to the suite click quietly and shortly afterwards I heard what I thought was crying.

I put a dressing-gown on and walked into the sitting room, when I put the light on I saw Christine sitting on the floor dressed as a sixteenth-century chamber-maid, with her back against the door laughing uncontrollably.

After a while I managed to get out of her what she was laughing at. It was this. A young Australian chap took a fancy to her during the party—he was handsome, well mannered and danced with her for most of the evening. He went to the buffet, brought her food and drink, then introduced her to most of the Melbourne socialites; he was the end in courtesy.

After the party, he asked if he could drive her home. He drove her to the Southern Cross Hotel, stopped his car outside—ran round to the nearside door and walked with her to the reception to get her key. He politely took the key, looked at the room number, pressed the elevator button to the eleventh floor, walked her to our room which was 1109, put the key in the lock and just as Christine was about to say "Thank you and good night," he put his arm across the door like a barrier and said: "Want sex?"

She has a great sense of humour and can relate a story as well as the best.

I joined in the laughter. Blossom woke up and wondered what the heck was going on. Soon she was laughing. We woke Anthony up and he joined in the fun. We rang room service for a couple of bottles of iced champagne and had another party of our own that went on till about five am.

Nowadays, if we are sitting at home watching a soap opera on television and the boy is trying to make the girl, invariably a voice from either me, Blossom or the kids will pipe up in an Australian accent: "Want sex?"

It was only a few months after this I remembered to ask her what her answer to "Want sex?" was. She started laughing again and told me that she said: "No—not tonight—thanks!"

From the Tivoli Theatre at Melbourne we moved to the Tivoli in Sydney. We all loved Sydney, we rented a house on the Harbour with swimming pool, barbecue, boats, etc. It was run by a family called Jackson. They had five kids of their own so with our brood there was always the babble of children either laughing, crying or fighting nearby. I would sit on the wall to fish, then sit and write either a song or some material for my act.

My fame from winning the Ivor Novello Award as Songwriter of the Year had followed me to Australia. I was asked by a well-known publisher if I had any ideas for a national Australian song—they had been looking for one for years to replace "Waltzing Matilda". I came up with words and music to a song called "A-U-S-T-R-A-L-I-A". I recorded it and it is played there quite regularly, it goes:

A-U-S-T-R-A-L-I-Ay,
The land of Koala
And the kangaroo
The billabong—the boomerang
The digeridoo
But wait a minute!
There's much more in it
They've got a whole lot of—people who say
"I'm so proud now
I'm one of the crowd now
In A-U-S-T-R-A-L-I-Ay"

A-U-S-T-R-A-L-I-Ay
From Darwin down to Melbourne
From Sydney to Perth
You'll get a welcome like you've never had on this
   earth
They'll shake your hand there
You'll feel grand there
They've got a whole lot of people who say
"I'm so proud now
I'm one of the crowd now
In A-U-S-T-R-A-L-I-Ay"

There are other verses, but that will give you an idea. It has a strong lilting melody. I have found that audiences love to hear their home town or country boosted and this particular song was a real flag waver. The Aussies would cheer when I did it in my act. I have been to Australia seven or eight times since that first trip for cabaret and this particular piece never fails to get them; it's like singing "Land of Hope and Glory" here in England. The only way to top it is to fill the stage with Union Jacks.

I was asked to play a night club in Sydney, called Chequers. It was run by a small Chinese named Denis Wong, a lovely little man with an unconscious humour—some of the things he has said have been handed all round the world.

Once he went to see the Beatles when they went to Sydney as quite a newish act. They appeared at the Stadium there. The kids in the audience were going wild, screaming, tearing seats, jumping up and down in ecstasy. Denis had been taken to see them by an agent hoping that he would book them at Chequers. He gazed round at this wild scene, then back at the Beatles on stage and said to the agent: "Okay, I like them—I take two!"

Another story attributed to Denis Wong: one of the chorus girls in the line was trying to fix her friend up with a job at his night club. "Please give my friend a job," she begged. "I'll think about it," promised Denis. After a few days he approached the girl who had asked him to fix her friend. "This girl," he said, "she a good dancer?" "Oh yes," gushed the girl. "She better dancer than you?" he smiled. "Yes, a lot better than me." Denis smiled more and said: "Okay, she hired—you fired!"

Once he walked into my dressing room and said: "Max, you sing 'Oss—stale—I—ay' tonight?" I said I would, adding "You like that song, don't you?" He said, "Cos I like—I bloody Ost—stalian, aren't I?"

When it was time to leave Australia, I thought it would be nice to have a holiday on the way back. I had told Jock not to book me any work until I told him I was ready—it was 1965 and I could not think of any time I had been able to have four consecutive weeks for a holiday. Two weeks was the most I had ever managed, there was always an engagement or broadcast or a TV show lurking, so I thought it might be nice for us to have four weeks in Honolulu—it was on the route back to England. We made arrangements to drop off there and stay at one of those lovely hotels along Waikiki Beach.

We chose the Hawaiian Village as the hotel to stay. It had everything, surf nearby, two pools, several restaurants, hula girls dancing, camera clubs, painting classes, it was a great hotel. The only trouble was, that on the first week, the bill came to £420.

I had been hit hard for Australian tax and couldn't see myself finding that sort of money for another three weeks so we'd have to find some place a bit cheaper. I bought the *Honolulu Advertiser* that evening and saw a house advertised for rent. It had five bedrooms, a pool and the hire of a station-wagon, all for £100 per week. It was twenty-odd miles from Waikiki so next day Bloss and I rented a car to take us out and have a look.

It was just what we wanted—the woman who wanted to rent it was going to Los Angeles for a month. She had three small children, so she understood about bringing kids with us. She was waiting for a divorce and her parting words were: "Treat it as your own—set fire to it, if you like!"

The next day we moved in with our entire tribe. Bob Dixon went on to London (I don't think he could take much more of our grand-children). We adored it. We were away from the holidaymakers and living among the real Hawaiians and what lovely people they are.

A dear friend of mine, Lou Levy, a music publisher from New York, asked me to call a friend of his who is a disc jockey-cum-radio-announcer-cum-father-confessor and has a four hour radio programme on a station known as KGMB in Honolulu—the name of this man is Aku.

Aku and I became good friends. Each morning, I would call him on the phone with a little anecdote that seemed to please his listeners. From this, lots of people listening would call me to say they had seen me in shows when they had been to London or on some of the American network TV shows I had done from New York and Los Angeles. He played my records continually and today I am as well-known in Honolulu as I am in Great Britain. In fact, one of the listeners phoning in asked that in view of my records being constantly played, KGMB should be called Keep Getting Max Bygraves. Thanks to Aku.

One day, with nothing to do, I noticed what a sorry state the house was getting into through not being looked after. Paint was peeling, doors were off hinges, windows were not closing. It was because the woman who rented it to us probably had not had a man about the house to do these odd jobs.

I decided to help. I went to the shops and bought a few tools, hammer, screw drivers, spanners and screws. I made a lot of the faults good again, then set to work on a rowing boat that we wanted to use but couldn't because one of the rowlocks was missing. A rowlock is what holds the oar, it allows you to get pressure on the oar.

I figured that if I inserted two six-inch screws about four inches apart, then bind the top of them with wire, it would work as a rowlock, we would then be able to row on the lagoon where the house was situated.

I did this and made a reasonable job of it—I put the boat into the lagoon and began to row out. When I was a couple of hundred yards out, the pressure was too much and the screws gave out. As I turned to pull in the oar on the side that had the good rowlock, the other oar slid into the water.

I was in a swim suit, so decided to jump in and retrieve it. It had wandered a good few yards from the row boat. The first thing I noticed as I got in the water was a very strong undercurrent, I am a fairly good swimmer and struck out for the boat, pushing the oar in front of me. I made the boat, panting like an old bull and threw the oar up into the boat.

If I can give advice at this stage, be guided by me and never try to get back into a rowing boat without somebody helping you. You will wear yourself out and find that it is practically impossible. There was no way I could get back in that row boat without up-ending it.

I yelled to my kids who were oblivious to me out there in the lagoon; they were playing records on a radiogram by the pool and could hear nothing. Meanwhile, I was getting weaker. I decided to swim, pushing the boat in front of me but it was heavy going in the current, also I was drifting farther and farther away from the house.

I yelled louder and louder but nobody could hear me, then I noticed I was drifting towards another large house—if I could steer towards this, it was about my last hope before I went out to sea. By some strength that I mustered I managed after what seemed a lifetime, to make the bottom of the garden of the house.

Nobody could hear my cry for help. I pulled myself up and as I did, my chest scraped on the coral. I got out and saw that I was bleeding from my neck down to my knees. As I lay there thankful to be where I was, out of the mess I had been in, down the garden lunged a great big Alsatian dog, all ready to turn me into a mid-morning meal.

"Oh Christ!" I thought, "please don't make me go back in that water." Luckily, there was a link chain fence that kept him away, the dog kept charging the fence. All I had to sit on was about eighteen inches of soil so his jowls were only a few inches from my face each time he charged.

I was still, for some reason that I have never figured out to this day, holding the rowing boat by the rope.

I had to make a decision, finish up as Pal Meat or get back in the boat. I pulled the boat as near as I could, then jumped in, just as the hound broke the fence. I hung on to the oar, ready to knock him senseless if he decided to jump too.

It took me ages and ages to manipulate that boat with one oar back to the house—eventually, I did it. I stepped off on to the little jetty, covered in blood which was flowing freely from my chest. I decided to get into the pool and wash it clean. As I was doing this,

Blossom came out, saw me in the pool, and said: "Come along, Max—lunch is ready. I've been calling you for an hour!" I thought: "Yes, and I've been bloody well calling you for two!"

When I got out of the pool she saw the blood and fainted. I got injected against the possibility of coral poisoning a little later and *I* fainted—I always do when I see a syringe going into my arm.

We left Hawaii looking bronzed and fit and rather sorry. I have been to Australia seven times since that first trip. I make it possible to stop off in Honolulu for a few days to enjoy the people, the climate and Aku, who I am glad to say is one of my dearest friends. He recently married a beautiful Hawaiian singer named Emma—they make a lovely couple.

I met the "top brass"
You could tell they had class
Back in those good old days.

They had me and my wife
On "This Is Your Life"
Back in those good old days.

I met Vidal Sassoon
The Prime Minister too
Noel Coward and of course the Oliviers.

Hartnell made me a tie
It's true, it's no lie
Back in those good old days.

When I got back to England I was asked to do another Command Performance. I had done so many by now that I was quite blasé about it. I was getting used to meeting Her Majesty, the Queen Mother and Prince Philip. I had done a dozen of them by now, two Royal Film Galas, plus a couple of private shows at Windsor Castle. The Queen always opened with: "It's nice to see you again." With each meeting I became freer and less tongue-tied.

In the spring of 1966, I was sitting in my office doing what I dislike most about my work, answering letters. My secretary, Jennifer, is wonderfully competent but there comes a time when they pile up from people who want personal replies. The letters come in different groups. First, I get a lot of requests to open fêtes or charity bazaars. I can get as many as thirty in a week. Should I be on television, with my face before the public, people are reminded to write so that figure could be even higher. I usually help where I can but it is impossible to do them all, hence the letters to the organisers. Secondly, there is a great demand for donations to different charities—a lot of these have to be refused too. Thirdly, there are songs from amateur songwriters who are convinced they have written the world's biggest hit, because they have been warned about plagiarism, they usually send their manuscript by registered post which has to be taken to a post office to be registered back. Very often Jennifer has to stand in a long queue to do this. Fourthly, fans write in for photographs which have to be personally autographed, "To Annie", "To Vera", "To Charles", etc. I get letters periodically asking me if I am Jewish. I never quite know how to handle these.

People also send me poems to put music to; ask advice on bringing up children; how to become a pop star; do I know what happened to so and so; and a dozen other subjects. One that I dread because it becomes so hard to reply, is to send some personal article to a charity to be auctioned. I have done it so often, I don't think I have anything left, I usually finish up now sending one of my latest LPs, autographed.

As I was saying, on this day I was sitting at my desk doing all this work when the telephone rang and somebody asked to speak to me. Before replying, I asked who it was speaking. "Buckingham Palace," they answered. I thought it must be Eric Sykes with a gag. I said: "Max Hargreaves speaking."

It *was* Buckingham Palace calling but I didn't know this, as far as I can remember, the conversation went on like this . . .

VOICE: "Are you Max Bygraves?"
ME: "Aye, lad—the one and only!"
VOICE: (after short silence) "Well—er—Her Majesty is having a private luncheon, just five or six people and she would like you to be her guest."
ME: "That's nice—what will we be eating—Spam?"
VOICE: "I'm sure we can find something you will enjoy."

At this stage, I suddenly became aware that it wasn't Eric Sykes —the more he spoke, the more I was convinced that this was pukka.

ME: "I'd be delighted—er, when?"
VOICE: "May 16th—12.45—if you can make it, I'll send you an invitation."

He hung up. I sat staring at the telephone. I was going to have lunch with the Queen. The first time I had ever seen her was when she was a little girl and I had sat on my father's shoulders in the Mall at her grandfather's Jubilee in 1935. I had waved my Union Jack at her and to this day I believed she had waved back at me, even though there were thousands of others there.

The next day, the invitation arrived—gilt-edged in an embossed envelope with "Buckingham Palace" printed on it. I had a small mews town house at the time in Belgravia, only half a mile from the Palace.

On the day I whistled a cab. It was a beautiful spring morning. "Palace, please," I said to the cabbie. We made our way towards Victoria then, instead of going towards St James' Park, he turned towards Hyde Park Corner. When he was half way down Piccadilly, I leaned forward and asked him where he was going. "Palace," he said, "Shaftesbury Avenue."

I shouted: "Not the Palace Theatre—Buckingham Palace!"

"Why the bleedin' hell didn't yer say so," he shouted back.

He dropped me at the main gates, I showed my invitation to a policeman who saluted and pointed to the archway I was to enter through. There were thousands of tourists with cameras. I could hear them clicking away as I walked alone across the courtyard. Most of them were from overseas and had no idea who I was but thought they had better take a picture in case I was something to do with Royalty. I walked with my hands clasped behind my back in royal fashion. Really, if you are a man it is the only thing to do with your hands.

The guards in their bearskins came smartly to attention as I passed through the arch and then quite suddenly I was in a court-yard with some steps leading up to Their Majesties' living part of the Palace.

I walked into this palatial oval hallway with a large oval carpet. In cabinets that were lit I could see rare and beautiful china.

A rather youngish, good looking man in a dark suit came forward, hand outstretched. "How nice of you to come—have a drink." He was an Equerry. He took me to a small table where a waiter in white bow tie and olive green coat mixed me a gin and tonic. I sipped it and was introduced to the rest of the luncheon party. There was Maurice Edelman, the Labour MP, and David Queensberry, who is now the Marquis of Queensberry and whose grandfather was part founder of the boxing rules. There was Mr Conway from the trade union, a viscount from the Admiralty, the Queen and Prince Philip and myself.

Two large doors opened and all that came through were two dogs, two Corgis. Both of them made for my feet. I bent down to play with them because they obviously wanted a game by their friskiness.

As I stood up, I heard a lady's voice say: "Chase them away if they are a nuisance!" I was looking right into the laughing eyes of our Queen. She was wearing a plain lemon dress with a simple gold brooch, she had a black patent handbag and shoes to match. She swung the handbag and rocked on the outside edges of her shoes very much like a schoolgirl does.

I had only seen her walk with dignity at all the "dos" I had seen her at—this was a revelation, it was so relaxing. In a few seconds everybody was at ease. She had two sherries; we talked about the weather, what dogs like to eat, what I was doing at the time, then we left the large reception room and walked into an adjoining room, rather small with an oval table set for lunch.

The plates were edged in green and gold. The cutlery was Kings pattern, the serviettes were of soft linen and we were served by fine looking men in olive green tailcoats and white ties, like the wine waiter who had served us at the reception.

We had consommé, followed by lamb with cauliflower cheese, then strawberries and cream, coffee and liqueurs, then we talked.

We were told the lunch would be over by 2.15 pm but we must have been a successful luncheon party because it was after three o'clock when we left. On the way out, David Queensberry asked me if I had a car with me. I said I hadn't, he offered me a lift, I expected to see a big Rolls or Daimler drive up, he took me over to a little red Mini that needed a good clean. As they opened the gates for us to drive through, I hid my face from the crowd, I didn't want to be recognised in this heap that he drove me home in.

For the rest of the year I went to Scotland to appear in a show, *Five past Eight*. This was produced by Dickie Hurran and really set Glasgow on fire. The Scots love a "live" show more than anybody else. I had a chance to excel: the sketches were good; the songs were great; and the accompanying band were the best I had worked with.

I played golf most days, fished or just drove the car up to the lochs and admired the breathtaking country. Weekends I would spend at Gleneagles. I brought my mother up for a two weeks' stay during the run. By now, you must have gathered that she likes Guinness. We stopped on a drive one day at a licensed restaurant that advertised afternoon teas.

Blossom and I were gasping for a pot of tea and assumed mum would be. "Tea?" I asked her. "No," she answered, "I'll have a Guinness—tea always keeps me awake." It was four o'clock in the afternoon.

It was during the run of *Five Past Eight* at the Alhambra Theatre in Glasgow that I began writing articles for newspapers.

The features editor of the *Scottish Daily Express* approached me with an idea. It was for an article on why an English comedian like myself could come up to Scotland and do well and yet so few of the Scots comedians could come south of the Border and make the same impact—he reckoned that since Harry Lauder and Will Fyffe, there had been practically none, in spite of Scotland at this very time having an abundance of fine, talented performers. The name of the features editor was Drew Rennie and he said he would "ghost" the article for me.

In my experience I have never found a reporter who can write jokes down with the same brevity and punctuation that an experienced comic can. Also a joke that is funny to tell does not always seem funny in print and vice versa. With this in mind, I asked him if he would mind me writing my own piece. He agreed and I told him I would let him have the five hundred words by the end of the day.

When I had completed the article, he sent a messenger to my hotel to pick it up.

It appeared next day and made quite an impression. There was good reaction to it and a few hours later Drew was on the phone asking me to write some more for which they were willing to pay me.

The Scots seemed to like my way of writing and I had a quarter page to myself on Fridays for the remaining ten weeks.

Furthermore, when I got back to London, the London *Evening News* had heard of my writing and asked me to do a series for them. At first I wrote them in collaboration with Spike Mullins but Spike had become busier and busier writing for some of the top comedians, so I had to go it alone. Time was also my enemy: writing is such a full-time job—furthermore, you need, to read to write well, to read books by people that matter.

I was keen on O. Henry, Damon Runyon, Thurber and Edgar Wallace, possibly because they wrote short pieces—that way it was possible to read them on a journey, or before retiring. Most of my reading today is *Punch* or *Readers' Digest* condensed volumes. Anyway, to give you an idea of what I was turning out in Scotland, perhaps the following will give you some indication; this was written after a cup final at Hampden Park and except for a little embroidery, it is more or less true.

CUP FINAL

Once, when I wanted to impress people what a brave chap I am, I used to say, quite nonchalantly, "I was in the Battle of Britain." Now I say: "I saw Rangers play Celtic."

A friend gave me a ticket for the Cup Final at Hampden Park

—at least I thought he was a friend. I now know I've got enemies who will stop at nothing.

Cunningly, I had worked it out that if I didn't wear a rosette for either Celtic or Rangers, I could watch the game as a neutral. What a mistake that was.

I took my seat between a sweet little old lady on one side and the Biggest Scotsman in the World on the other.

The B.S. in the W. produced a bottle of Highland Dew—took a swig and passed it to me. "Take a drap, laddie, it's good for the larynx." I did as I was told. "Give ye're old mother a drink—what sort of a son are ye?"

Without comment, I passed it to the sweet little old lady, she almost emptied it.

The B.S. in the W. then announced in a loud voice he was aware that the mentally deficient, born out of wedlock on the other side of the ground had only brought their eleven hooligans along to cause trouble on the pitch, but, decent people would see that they didn't get away with it.

I had to have another swig and drink on that, a subtle blend of metal polish and vitriol that "Mother" produced from her shopping bag. "Sassenachs!" she snarled, her bonnet quivering. "Aye," we nodded. I gave thanks that I had a masterly command of the Scots tongue. We had another drap.

The whistle blew for off—just in front of me a small group had started up a chorus of "Mother Machree". What really happened, I don't know, but the sweet little old lady who had just finished the bottle, threw it at the choral society, whether the brew had made her aim unsteady, I can't remember, but the empty bottle hit a police inspector in the back of the neck so that he lost all interest in the game.

"Mother," said the giant with great admiration, "you've killed a policeman." She smiled sweetly, like a little girl winning a party competition.

"She's a fine woman, your mother."

"Aye," I nodded again.

At half time the Hercules produced another full one. I was already feeling "sloshed" but even through the haze it suddenly occurred to me that if "them" over there felt towards us like we did towards them, then, this could turn into something that would make Bannockburn look like a Girl Guides' picnic. What chance would a lone Sassenach have?

The giant was looking at me with new interest. "Ye ken, Jock, ye've got an awfee familiar face."

That did it.

"I'm awa to the lavatory," I said, "Look after mother."

As I climbed the stairs to leave the ground, it suddenly dawned on me that I was wearing a blue suit similar to the blue of the Rangers rosettes and a green tie that St Patrick would have adored. As I felt every eye turn towards me, fate stepped in.

"Mother" with another empty had just got her second policeman on the pitch and I managed to get out of the ground with the "Hampden Roar" ringing in my ears.

Journalistically, they didn't set Fleet Street on fire but they gave me a lot of pleasure writing them. A few people wrote and told me they had enjoyed them too. This gave me a great deal of delight.

At one time I did consider going to one of those tax haven countries to enable me to work outside Britain and keep most of my earnings. Also I visualised myself writing a book once a year to keep my hand in, then perhaps one day I might blossom into a good writer.

I thought about it but I really couldn't come up with any country that could offer what this overtaxed, overpopulated, strike bound, but uncorrupt little island could offer.

I am British—I like being British. I wish our ancestors had put us a little nearer the Equator—I don't like the winters, that's why most years now I play dates abroad, but I am British Bwana—always will be Comrade! And to the Union Jack, I raise my fez!

By now I was getting offers to appear all over the world. After Scotland I accepted an engagement in Hong Kong at the Mandarin Hotel, probably, at that time, the best hotel in the world. I took Anthony with me.

I liked having Anthony with me—he was always good company and had become a proficient drummer. He had studied for almost three years and was ready to start making a living. He was about eighteen and I knew that seeing the rest of the world could only be good for him.

He surprised me in many ways. First, he was a far better musician than I had imagined. Not only that, he would come forward from the drums and do a routine with me that took in juggling, dancing and joke-telling—on all of these subjects he was OK and the audience were always won over by him.

Second, I saw him for the first time as a man. I remember one day being invited by the owner of the hotel to go on his boat.

There were several local people on board and among them a young, beautiful girl that Bob, Jock and I thought was a "cracker". She looked about twenty and every one of us would have liked to have asked her for her telephone number. That evening when it was time to go to the cabaret room I knocked on Anthony's door along the corridor. It was answered by the girl on the boat. On the way to the cabaret room I thought to myself for the first time in my life, "Max, you're getting older!"

From Hong Kong, Anthony and I went to Japan. Before we left Hong Kong we were told by an import and export agent to get some duty free whisky. In Hong Kong at that time it was about £1 a bottle but in Tokyo it cost £17 a bottle. We were allowed three bottles each, so Anthony and I purchased six bottles between us. What for, I didn't really know—I never touched whisky. What's more six bottles were very heavy, but we took his advice and arrived in Tokyo with them.

I loved the Japanese. I couldn't believe that these people could have committed the atrocities I had read about or seen in films like *Bridge on the River Kwai*. They were courteous, clean, obliging, they resented tipping and served with a smile. We became tourists, visiting all the places of interest. The Olympics had been held there recently and the city had inherited some fine buildings.

One of the things we decided to do because it seemed a "must" for Westerners, was to have a Japanese bath, by a Japanese girl, in a Japanese bath-house. We made enquiries and settled for one quite near the hotel.

We arrived at a reception like any doctor's surgery—there was a pretty receptionist who bowed and asked us to undress in a room covered by a curtain. Both a little shy, not knowing what to expect but grinning from ear to ear, we undressed. Into the room came another pretty girl, by now we were both down to our briefs. "Take beliefs off," she said in English. We did this. "You flends?" she asked. I said in the same sort of English, "He no flend—he number one son!" Looking straight at our private parts, a bigger smile came over her face. "Ah! Can see!"

What she saw, I have never figured out. We were shown into a large tiled bath and just sat there for ten minutes or more. Then three naked Japanese gentlemen came in and got in with us. One read the paper which he kept above the water all the time.

The girl walked in, told Anthony and me to get out. She handed us a little three-legged stool, like a miniature milking stool and then proceeded to lather us with a large sponge. She did us all over but handed us the sponge to do our own private work.

We were then swilled down with buckets of tepid water and wrapped in enormous crisp white towels, after this we were laid on a massage table. A girl went to work on me, so gently that I fell fast asleep. The next thing I knew was looking up at Anthony, fully dressed who was saying: "Come on, dad—you can't sleep here." I got up, dressed, paid the bill and walked back to the hotel feeling great.

That same evening we went to a Geisha house, to be fed and entertained in the Japanese manner.

We were bowed in by the lady of the house, then shown to a room where four young girls were on their knees with foreheads touching the floor. After we were seated on the floor with our legs under the table, they began to serve delicious food.

I had read Ian Fleming's article in the *Sunday Times* and remembered how he had raved about raw fish in Japan. When it was brought in, it looked awful. I had been enjoying the food up till then but this raw fish was not for my palate. With all the girls sitting there watching us, I didn't know what to do with what I had in my mouth. I knew if I swallowed it, I would be ill. So behind my serviette I asked Anthony to ask one of the girls where the loo was situated. I got up and got rid of it but I couldn't get rid of the nausea it had brought. It spoiled my dinner and made me queasy. Because of that I decided to never read anything more by Ian Fleming.

When I felt alright again we drank Sake, warmed on a small flame. Then one of the girls got what looked like a balalaika and proceeded to sing—she had a sweet little voice and because of the wine and the company, they could have dropped another atom bomb and we wouldn't have cared.

Anthony happened to remark how much the sound of the instrument being played sounded like a ukelele. On the word ukelele one of the girls' eyes lit up—she left the room and returned a few minutes later holding a real Hawaiian ukelele. I tuned it up and went into "Somebody Stole my Gal". The girls went wild with excitement. Anthony picked up two chopsticks and gave me a rhythm accompaniment. Suddenly the room was full of Geisha girls from other rooms, all laughing and asking for requests of Western songs: "Sunny side of the street", "Bye, bye blues" and many others.

They were reluctant to let us go but it had gone three am and we were leaving next day. I asked for the bill, which they had greatly reduced because of the entertainment we had given them.

I felt for my wallet but it wasn't there. I had left it in another suit when I had changed for the evening. The owner was unconcerned and told me to forget it—the lot only came to about £8 but I felt guilty at not paying—these people had entertained us for about seven hours.

We got in a taxi which took us to the Okura Hotel where we were staying. I rushed up to the room, got my wallet and also picked up the six bottles of Johnny Walker Black Label we had brought from Hong Kong. Anthony waited in the taxi and we drove back to the house again. I gave the lady the money in Japanese yen and then presented her with the six bottles of whisky. She fell to the floor kissing my feet: this particular whisky was fetching £20 a bottle at that time. She was still bowed with her head to the ground when the taxi was half a mile up the road.

The East made such an impression on Anthony that on the way back, when we stopped over for a few days in Hawaii, he said he would like to go back to Hong Kong where he thought he could get a job with a band. There and then he turned back to go via Tokyo and I left Honolulu for London—we shook hands at the airport and he eased the moment by saying, "I'll get off at Tokyo to see if that Japanese lady has got up from kissing the ground you and Johnny Walker walked on." Then he was gone.

When I got back to my house at Leatherhead, it seemed very empty. Apart from Blossom, the house was still. Christine had gone back to Melbourne. She was working as a beautician in one of the large stores there. She had taken her two children with her. We had regular letters from her. She told us she had met an Australian artist named Barry Green and had become engaged.

Anthony was in Hong Kong and was determined to make his own career. Maxine had moved into her own "pad" in London, so this left Bloss and me to use five bedrooms and five bathrooms. A short while before we had been full up, now we were wondering what to do with all the room we had. Never had it been so quiet in our abode.

I had a nice offer to go to South Africa, so I took it. I did not know what to expect in South Africa. I had heard lots of conflicting stories about apartheid. I had a drummer who was warned by his union not to accompany me so, after working for me for several years, we had to part company. He did not want to ruin his chances of work in England in case he was blacklisted. He was newly wed and had a baby son so I couldn't blame him. Strange thing is that after refusing to go with me he got a job on one of the cruise ships, landed in South Africa, fell in love with the place and now has his home there. He is one of the top drummers there and makes three times what he made in England, with a home of his own, a big car and very little taxes.

The South Africans loved our particular show. They packed the place each evening. They opened their homes to us and we received more hospitality there than any other land we had been to.

I couldn't get over the fact that in Johannesburg the miners who mined the earth's richest mineral could be so poorly paid. There were lots of excuses given about how well they were doing compared with other black states but it nagged at me. As a matter of fact it was the only part of South African policy that did irk me. People in England had spoken of the troubles there but it was one of the very few places I had been to that had *no* troubles.

Britain was having student demonstrations that were getting beyond a joke. There was "Paki-bashing" going on in towns all over the country.

America was having riots in the South; President Kennedy and Martin Luther King had been assassinated; there were buses and schools being burned.

France was going through a democratic upheaval. The only place *not* having troubles was South Africa and to be perfectly honest I was enjoying the audiences, the social life, the golf courses and the sunshine.

One day I was asked to play in a golf foursome; it was a friendly match between three professionals and myself. I was to partner Bobby Locke, the great Bobby Locke that is. We were to play against Brian Barnes and Hedley Muscroft, two pros from England who were there competing in the South African Open. I was playing to a sixteen handicap and playing rather well.

They had arranged to play for a lot more money than I usually played for. The most I ever play for is five pounds, mostly for a pound or a couple of balls. They had ten pounds on the first nine, ten on the second and ten on the game, then five pounds for birdies and ten pounds for eagles. The money didn't worry me too much but I didn't want to be responsible for Bobby Locke shelling out because I had let him down.

We managed to win the first nine holes which put us ten pounds ahead. Bobby had three birdies and we were well in front.

At the seventeenth Bobby hit a lovely shot up the fairway. It was my turn to hit his ball next. As I got up to it I could see it was teed up on the grass just waiting to be struck. We were all square on the second nine holes. I took my four wood from the bag and weighed up the next shot.

"What have you got there, Master?" Bobby asked.

"A four wood."

"A four wood's too much, Master—you'll go through the green."

"What shall I use then?"

"Take your five wood," said the great one.

"I haven't got a five wood."

"Here, use mine."

He handed me his five wood and I squared up to the ball. I needed to get about one hundred and fifty yards. I took careful aim and swung. Everything was in my favour—it was the greatest golf stroke I had ever played. The ball sailed on to the green, ran thirty yards and stopped four inches from the hole. Brian, Hedley, Bobby and all the caddies applauded. Bobby walked up, tapped it in and we won the hole. We halved the eighteenth and our opponents paid us forty-five pounds each.

In the clubhouse later Bobby said, "You must have a five wood in your bag, Master, it's a club you cannot do without." I said I would get one when I got back to England. Bobby asked me to leave it to him. He arranged that I should go into Lillywhites at Piccadilly Circus when I returned, see the manager and ask for a Bobby Locke Number Five Wood. He was going to write ahead and make sure it would be there for me. I thanked him and promised I would go in, then we bought drinks all round with our winnings.

We appeared in Durban, Cape Town, Port Elizabeth and East London. Every town gave us a tumultuous welcome. Every town had "standing room only" boards out. Bob Dixon liked the beer and found lots of company in BOAC aircrews and the enormous English population there. Then we returned to England.

After I had been back two or three weeks I happened to be passing Lillywhites in London. I wondered whether I should go in and ask the manager whether he'd had word from Bobby Locke about the club I was supposed to pick up. I thought it might look rather rude if I didn't, yet on the other hand if Bobby had forgotten it might seem out of order—I decided to go and ask.

The salesman was all smiles. "Yes, Mr Bygraves, we know all about it," he said as he produced a gleaming number five wood with the famous Bobby Locke signature on. "Here, sir—shall I wrap it?" I waited whilst he cleverly wrapped it in brown paper then sellotaped it up. "There you are, sir," he smiled, "that will be eight pounds fifteen!" I paid him the money, muttering something about next time I see Bobby Locke I'll tell him to stuff his number five woods, after all I had won him forty-five pounds. I could have bought it from the pro at my own course.

What made matters more exasperating was that I had come to London without the car and had to go back to Leatherhead in the rush hour on the train with this golf club under my arm.

I managed to find a carriage I could just get into. It was jammed with commuters so I had to hold the club well back in case it "goosed" some lonely spinster who would pull the communication cord.

"Mind the doors!" shouted a Jamaican railway porter and slammed the carriage door closed, right onto the head of my new golf club that was sticking out a bit too much.

When I got out at Leatherhead, I removed the brown paper to see what damage the door closing on the club had done. The head was hanging by the waxed cotton.

I had been back in England for a few weeks when another offer came to go back to Australia. I accepted and took Blossom with me. We stayed at our favourite haunt by the waterfront at Sydney Harbour. I was to play Chequers again for a four week season. In the middle of the engagement I had a phone call from Jock telling me my father was seriously ill. I asked to be let off for six or seven days and did the return trip to London. This was the most exhausting week I had ever experienced. The flight to London is a marathon from Sydney. Blossom had stayed on in Australia for the week I was to be away. On 14 January 1968, I landed at Heathrow in severe winter weather. I had just left ninety-two degrees the day before. I went straight to the hospital at Abbey Wood in Kent, was shown to the ward and there was my dad in bed breathing heavily, riddled with cancer, looking up at me with only slight recognition. The body he had been so proud of most of his life had wasted down to about seventy pounds. I held his hands and felt the messages he was trying to send through them. They were cold but I held them tight and during that period I lived all the things we had done together—football in the park with both our coats as goalposts; walks down the Lane on Sunday mornings; the cuddles and affection when I was off colour. After a few hours he died. It was the dawn of 15 January. It seemed he had hung on to spend that last meeting with me. My mother, brother and sisters all wept.

There were lots of arrangements to be made—death certificates, funeral arrangements, journeys to and from the hospital. He was buried at the small cemetery in Welling, and that night I got the plane back to Sydney.

I continued the engagement at Chequers but was very depressed —there were things I did in my act that reminded me so much of my father. He loved the song "You Need Hands"—he was quite proud of the fact I had written it and although he was never a show-off, he couldn't resist telling people I was the composer. As I sang it I could feel the emotion welling up inside me. I was never so happy to finish a date. Especially with the flight fatigue, Sydney to London, then back again—all in one week.

We took the journey home steadily, stopping off at Fiji for five days' rest. We stayed at the Fijian Hotel—a very nice residence on the edge of the sea. I liked the Fijians who were a cheerful lot. The hotel was run very efficiently by an Irishman whose name I forget.

We became the proper tourists. I dare not trust Blossom with the camera—she just has no idea how one works. She thinks a box camera is for taking pictures of boxes. You only have to see some of the photos she has taken of me in different parts of the world to appreciate how hopeless she is with a Pentax.

However, on this day I recall we invested in a trip to one of the other islands, it was about an hour by boat.

The boat was a modern fishing launch that held about ten of us trippers. Our fellow travellers were all Americans.

We ploughed our way through the swirling Pacific to this outer island. When we landed we saw the natives living almost in the same way as they had lived for the past thousand years. The huts were mud, and there was a king or witch doctor who gave us some liquid to drink that tasted like lighter fuel; my lips actually became numb as I sipped it.

In the huts the natives made material from bark. They sold it to us for table place mats. We bought everything they offered—beads —shells—musical instruments etc., etc.

We were shown the sacred prawns in water so clear it was like highly polished crystal. We ate our packed lunches on the beach and at three pm we made our way back to the mainland. We should have been back by four pm or soon after. On the way back I asked the skipper what a thing was that was blowing in the breeze. It had coloured ribbons on with a hook like a butcher uses to hang meat.

"It's a spinner," he said. He then took it down and gave it to me to inspect. "Here I'll show you how it works." He took the large spinner and connected it to the line of one of the large rods with enormous chromium reels such as those used by fishermen for shark fishing. He trailed it into the water saying "We might get a bite."

We watched the spinner bobbing up and down in the boat's wake a while, then lost interest and talked amongst ourselves. All of a sudden one of the crew shouted "Strike!" Everywhere action began, the boat slowed down as the skipper cut the engines, he raced to a chair at the back of the boat, put the rod in a hole between his legs and let the reel out with a whirring sound. He then strapped a harness across his body and sat there, shoulders hunched, winding slowly now and then. We all came down to the back of the boat to see what sort of a fish was on the end of the line. After several minutes the fish surfaced and threshed a good fifteen feet out of the water. "Jesus Christ!" said the skipper. "This is a *big* one!"

It was too—it was the biggest fish I have ever seen. A marlin; the guess was that it weighed somewhere in the region of five hundred pounds. It was imperative the skipper land it because at that time Fiji was selling itself as a tourist attraction. A picture of this fish in one of the world's fishing magazines would have brought some of those prosperous deep sea fishermen down there on the first available planes.

He played it and played it. It began to get dark. It had been almost two hours since we had made the strike, the boat was rolling along at about two knots and most of us were beginning to feel seasick. The skipper couldn't have cared less, he wanted that marlin. He kept grunting things like, "Come on, baby—come to daddy."

Now I began to feel seasick and it wasn't long before I gave my packed lunch back to the sea. I felt awful. Blossom was crying with sickness—every American was rolling about groaning, but the skipper hung on. They put a searchlight on and through the beam we could see the fins of dozens of sharks. It was frightening: out there in the dark with a half crazed skipper and more sharks than I had seen bloaters. They were actually banging against the boat, waiting for the marlin to give up so as they could go in for the kill and nuzzle it to death.

After what seemed a lifetime, it got nearer the boat. With only about thirty feet of line separating the marlin from the boat we all came on deck to watch it being "gaffed".

The marlin seemed about as long as the boat we were on. After a lot of manœuvring, they managed to get it near the boat. As the crewman got it even nearer he cut the line too soon and the half dead marlin rolled back into the sea. After almost five hours of fishing we had lost the prize they were after.

The sharks went mad as they furiously attacked the half dead body of the marlin. The skipper shook with exasperation as we watched the boat pull slowly away from what would have been one of the biggest fish landed in Fiji. He then put his head in his hands and cried like a baby. We all stood silent.

In another half hour we were anchoring in the small harbour by the hotel. Nobody spoke: we just wanted to get to our rooms, get showered and then to bed.

My legs were like jelly from the seasickness. I helped Blossom on to the quayside, she looked green, I went to the bar to get a brandy to settle me and she went off to bed.

As I walked into the bar in a pair of swim trunks and open neck shirt the head waiter came up and said, "Sorry, sir, but nobody allowed in bar after six o'clock without jacket and necktie." I told him to "P--- off", walked to the bar and ordered a double brandy then I had the same again and felt much better. Then I left to go up to bed.

I must explain that the hotel rooms were built rather like tenements. There were six floors and on each floor were doors painted different colours, blue, green, red, yellow and so on. Ours was a green door on the fifth floor, there was no lift and I walked up the stairs to our landing on the fifth.

The key was in the lock; when I entered Blossom was already in bed with the sheet pulled over her head, she didn't even stir as I walked in. I took my shoes off quietly and decided against a shower. I was completely exhausted and thought it would be better to just clean my teeth then go to bed.

I tiptoed into the bathroom so as not to wake Blossom. When I got in there I noticed something that didn't quite dawn on me at first. There were different coloured toothbrushes and strange looking brands of toothpaste. There were also women's things on a line that did not belong to Blossom. As I gathered my thoughts I suddenly realised I was not in my own room. I had walked up one floor less and I was actually in the room immediately below ours. As this dawned on me I thought I'd better get out of it.

I picked up my shoes that I had taken off beside the figure I had thought was Blossom and quietly crept out, closing the door gently behind me, I walked up another flight and into the room that was ours and went to bed. This time I checked to see if it was my wife in the next bed.

On the following day we were leaving for San Francisco. The manager had promised to drive us the twenty miles to the airport to catch the plane. On the way he talked about the happenings of the day before. "Oh geeze," he said, "everything went wrong yesterday—I've got trouble with one of the staff and I don't know which one it is." I asked him what sort of trouble, he said, "Last night one of the natives got into one of the guests bedrooms and tried to rape her—he sat on her bed, took his shoes off and then went into the bathroom, he couldn't find anything worth taking so he left. I'll have to find out who it is because I had such faith in all of them—but of course I can't have him wandering round these spinsters' bedrooms."

I was only listening with half an ear, then suddenly it dawned on me what he was saying. "That wasn't one of the native boys—that was me!"

"You?" he asked.

"Yes." I told him what had happened the night before, how I had gone into the wrong room and how I had crept out again.

When we got to the airport he rushed me to a call box and dialled the hotel number. He asked for the room of the lady I was supposed to have raped. When she answered he gave me the phone, "Tell her what happened." I made my apologies and told her I was sorry for the trouble I had caused. She accepted the explanation in somewhat dismal tones. I had ruined one of her finest hours.

We flew on to San Francisco, stayed a few days then on to New York for a few more days, then on to London.

I had told Jock not to accept any more offers because I really felt like having a month or more off, but after a week I got restless.

One Monday evening I was sitting at home watching television when the phone rang—the operator asked me if I would accept a personal call from Dallas, Texas, USA. I said I would and a voice at the other end explained that a Texan had seen me in cabaret at Hong Kong and would "like me to come to Dallas and give the people there my kind of humour".

"Alright, when would you like me there?"

"Next Saturday."

"Huh? That's only three or four days away!"

"Yeah—that's right!"

"How long for?"

"For one night!"

"I can't come for one night to Texas," I said.

"We'll give you ten thousand dollars and pay all expenses."

"I'll be there!" I said.

The voice said an agent would bring me tickets, half the money in advance, hotel reservations, etc., the following day.

Sure enough a courier turned up at my offices with all the documents as promised. Bob, Jock and I left Heathrow Airport at ten am, Friday morning; we changed at New York and got a plane to Dallas that arrived at three am at Dallas Airport.

Waiting for us in the dry heat was a nine-seater air-conditioned Cadillac. The chauffeur was in full livery. He drove us to the Dallas Sheraton Hotel, where a staff of bell boys had been kept on to take our bags to the rooms.

Bob Dixon is difficult to impress. It's hard to believe he was born in a small town like Ulverston, Lancs, and not be moved by some of the happenings through our partnered years. On the plane, he had been saying how angry he was because he had forgotten his transistor radio. He had taken it all round the world but on this trip he had forgotten it.

The Cadillac, the bell boys, impressed him not in the slightest—

he was still missing his "tranny", a word he had taken from the Aussies.

We were each given a suite in the penthouse. Bob was the first to be shown into his, this was called the Colonial Suite, a palatial apartment done in early American style, there were lawn-green chairs covered in daffodil yellow cushions, ankle-deep carpets, sumptuous sofas and a large oval bed in the bedroom. He wandered in, hands in pockets, but his eyes were searching for a radio; he couldn't see one. "Are you alright?" I asked him. "Yes—it will be alright," he replied mournfully.

I went to my suite and began to unpack—I had a shower and was about to dry myself when there was a knock on my door. Ringing wet from the shower, I put a towel round me and answered it. I opened it to see Bob all smiles. "It's in the headboard." I looked at him: "What's in the headboard?"

"The switch for the radio," he said.

"Oh—well, you alright now?"

"Yeah—good hotel isn't it?"

He would lie awake all night listening to the local news until the early hours, then get up about noon for breakfast. It's his way of life and I never interfere. He has never been late for a cue or a performance.

We did the show in the evening. The guests of honour were Princess Alexandra and her husband, the Rt Hon. Angus Ogilvy. It was most successful.

After the show, we had drinks with them and were then invited by a Mr Marcus, who is the owner of Neiman Marcus, one of the world's largest stores, to keep the Cadillac for the following day and go for a tour of the city.

The car called for us about eleven am and the chauffeur asked us where we would like to go. Jock asked if we could go along the route where President Kennedy had been assassinated. "Yes, Sir," he said in that Southern drawl. He was without doubt the politest American I have ever met. We were called "Sir" all the time. We were referred to as "gentlemen". In fact, I should think he called everybody a gentleman—men that is.

As we drove down Elm Street past the Book Depository, where Lee Oswald had hidden to kill the President, the chauffeur who was giving us a commentary was saying: "Here is Elm Street—here is the actual spot where the President was hit and that window up on the left there is where the *gentleman* pulled the trigger."

There was a deathly silence in the car—it was hard to believe that on a Sunday morning in this peaceful setting, this dastardly crime could have taken place. The church bells tolled as we got out of the car, walked up to the rooms, picked up our cases, left for the airport and were back in England the same evening, with ten thousand dollars in my pocket, plus the memory of an unusual weekend.

The following summer of that year I went for a season at the Princess Theatre, Torquay.

I loved Torquay. Although it was a long distance from London I liked it enough to buy a house there. The show was a huge success and I spent most of the day out on a boat that I also purchased locally. If I wasn't on the boat, I was on the golf course with Dickie Henderson who was appearing at another theatre in town.

One of the gags I did in that show was this. In my first entrance I would tell the audience they had better be in a good mood because if the manager saw anybody in the audience not laughing, they would be thrown out immediately. I then proceeded to tell a joke, at the finish of the joke I would ask the electrician to put the theatre lights up to see if everybody was laughing. The manager would co-operate with the joke and come walking down the aisle to see who was and who wasn't laughing, then from the stage I would point out a man who wasn't—this was Bob Dixon who had been "planted" in the same seat every night.

The manager would see the way I was pointing, call two burly attendants who had truncheons (papier mâché) they would then drag him out of his seat in full view of the audience and frog march him out of the theatre as they beat him with the truncheons.

It was a great opening to the show and got roars of laughter as I carried on saying, "Now you know what to expect if you don't laugh!"

One night after the show had been running for several weeks I did the joke the same way as I did it every show. I couldn't see too clearly because of the spotlights in my eyes. I pointed to the seat but there was another face in place of Bob's. As the attendants pretended to beat him, I heard a voice shouting like a small child: "Daddy—daddy—don't let them beat me—I've travelled eight thousand miles to see you!"

It was Anthony—he had been in Hong Kong for over a year and returned without telling anybody. I couldn't believe my eyes or ears. I just stood there looking at him, I couldn't even think of any lines to say. I just stood on the stage with my mouth open.

I found out afterwards he had arrived in Torquay just before the show started and arranged with Bob to swop places with him— good thing I have a strong constitution—I think I would have collapsed if I hadn't.

So Anthony was back with us. Then we had an air mail from Christine to say she was going to marry her Australian beau, Barry Green, and afterwards they were coming overland with her two children to England; they would be with us in six months!

Maxine in the meantime had got fed up with the pad in town so she also returned. Suddenly, Leatherhead was full up again. All the Bygraves were together again.

The entertainment industry had become revolutionised. Each month brought more permissiveness. The Beatles and Carnaby Street were what swinging England was all about. Flower Power had come in with a vengeance. It was a great opportunity to "drop out" if you were a young person. Hair got longer; trousers got wider; people looked unkempt. They wore beads; gave up marriage; the girls were on the Pill; jokes got cruder; songs became nonsensical; television had plays with no endings: you had to find the message hidden in there somewhere.

Suddenly the West End of London and most other cities were catering for fellows in dirty raincoats who walked up and down the equivalent of Soho gazing at the unbelievable pictures of nudes showing outside all the little cinemas that had opened again.

I wrote a song for myself that I included in my act that got big belly laughs. It will give you some idea of what was making them laugh back in 1969.

"PERMISSIVE SOCIETY"

Words and music by Max Bygraves

This is the age of permissive society
Cannabis, resin and pot
Forget all you learned about proper propriety
Soon you'd have seen all the lot.

Just off Leicester Square is a show they call "Hair"
It's groovey, it's "with it", it's rocky
The boys are as naked as when they were born
Except they are now twice as cocky.

I went to a film it was called "Sister George"
Concerning the opposite sex
The things that they do used to be so taboo
And they gave it Certificate X
This "George" is a woman she lives with a girl
Explain that to me if you please
There were no sub-titles—I got in a whirl
I don't understand Lebanese.

A few weeks ago I was in Amsterdam
Where Yoko and John were on view
I was in the hotel so I went to their room
Just to say to them "How do you do"
They both were in bed—I got quite a surprise
They both had white nighties on
I said "Hello Yoko"—she lifted her eyes
And said "I'm not Yoko—I'm John"!

I would imagine there comes a time in most people's lives when they arrive at a crossroads; a decision has to be made that can make or break.

I remember being asked to speak at the Press Council Office, just off Fleet Street. The guests of honour were five millionaires, they were Paul Getty, Paul Chambers of ICI, Bernard Delfont, Billy Butlin and Lord Bernstein of Granada.

The idea was for them each to speak for five minutes and tell the journalists assembled how they made their first million.

It was most interesting and each one agreed there was that one minute in their lives that had they made a wrong decision, they wouldn't have made that million.

They are all clever men and would obviously have done it at some other time, but, as I say, they took the right decision at the right moment and in each case it made them very rich. The decision I had to take at this stage of my career was to go on television for long periods.

Television is not very kind to stage performers. They are usually too "big" for the small screen. It is very entertaining to see a star from the theatre once in a while but see them every week and you can be bored very quickly. See somebody like Liza Minelli once or twice a year—it's great; put her on every week and that energy is too much.

Strangely enough, it is the mini-personalities who do well on TV. All our big TV stars today were never bill toppers before they went "on the box".

Morecambe and Wise were always a supporting act, so was Harry Worth, so were Charlie Drake, Eric Sykes, Terry Scott and several others—they became bill toppers from constant exposure.

All of these artistes were given time to develop by the BBC. They allowed them to blossom over two or three years. Some didn't make it but the ones I have just mentioned did. The BBC could afford to slot them in some quiet spot between six and seven pm then, when the time was right, launch them into a long running series in peak periods, when they were ready and experienced.

Then with their usual foolishness, the BBC lost them to ITV because they hadn't had the foresight to sign them up in advance. Usually ITV reaped all the harvest from these performers—they could always lure them over because they could pay more.

The Beeb loves to plead poverty, it always has done, but with one of the men I mentioned in charge—Getty, Delfont, Bernstein, Butlin, Chambers—I would bet my life they could come up with profits rather than keep putting up licence fees.

For instance, it is beyond me why the Army and the Navy take space on Independent Television and plough our tax money into the pockets of private enterprise when we have a government corporation that could give six or seven minutes exposure each evening and take the same rates. Why do British Rail and British Airways have to pay fantastic fees to advertise to the public when we own a department that can get to as many people as ITV, in some cases more? It doesn't have to get in the way of programmes either, just two minutes at the beginning of peak programmes would save the tax payer thousands and thousands. Anyway, I don't want to talk about that because I could go on for reams. I was telling you about me at the crossroads.

My dilemma was this—to be off television was to be out of show business: the public believed if you weren't on the small screen, you were starving in some attic. On the other hand, if I did go on would I be able to come up with a show that would be acceptable week after week? If I wasn't good I would be relegated to a later hour—advertisers wouldn't advertise. This could hurt my box office appeal. It had to be good from the start.

I had had many offers to star in a series—then one day when the "boss man" Phillip Jones phoned through as he had been doing on and off for months, I said I would like to go on Thames TV for him.

I was given a very competent director named Bill Stewart, a bit flash, but otherwise a nice guy. I had found a writer who I thought could have been the best in the land if he had a little more confidence in himself: Spike Mullins. The orchestra we chose was Geoff Love, one of the best decisions I ever made. We decided to call the show simply *Max*.

It happened right from the first moment—we had lots of good ideas. I was able to draw from a wealth of experience. The patter and sketches were original and we topped or nearly topped the ratings every week.

Geoff Love endeared himself to the viewers. I had guests like Aimi MacDonald and Beryl Reid, Danny la Rue and it was a big hit.

I followed this up with another series which did equally well. Spike Mullins had gained great confidence and was writing superb lines. Just to give you an idea, the following is a sample of his work, it was written seven years ago and sometimes I bring it out in a routine that never fails to get big laughs and sounds as modern as today's.

"I was having an argument with my wife a few weeks ago—we have little arguments—sometimes she wins—sometimes I win—this time she lost—which was a pity, 'cos she had lovely teeth. The argument was this . . . I was reading the paper, and there was an article on women who, when their families grow up, like to go out to work—to occupy themselves . . . So I said to her, 'Why don't you get a job?'—and she said: 'Why don't *you*?' You can never have a sensible discussion with her. She had the old excuse that by the time she had done the washing and ironing —then delivered it—she was too tired. She said, 'What I need is a holiday—let's go on a cruise—round the Mediterranean— let's have a second honeymoon . . . it will be different.' I said, 'How do you mean—different?' She said, 'Well, this time we won't take the kids.'

So I booked a cruise with a German steamship line called Vitner
—Schmitler—and Eichmann. The name of the boat was the SS
Lucy Canyon—the front half belonged to the *Lusitania*, and the
back half to the *Torrey Canyon* . . . I don't know where they got
the middle bit, but our cabin had a periscope . . .

The SS *Lucy Canyon*—the SS was for sentimental reasons—it was
the Captain's old regiment.

As soon as my son Anthony saw it, his hair turned white—and
he only came to see us off.

I'll never forget the day we left Southampton—there was a crowd
of people on the quay waving and cheering—that's the last we
saw of the crew.

We had to wait until we were three miles out from land before
we could buy duty free cigarettes—and six days without a smoke
is a long time . . .

There was a little shop on board where you could buy essentials
like life-belts, distress rockets, water.

One night there were about eight of us on deck, and we went
for a moonlight swim—the rail collapsed. But we got back
alright—the Captain put a searchlight on us and threatened to
open fire.

Then one of the passengers was awarded a medal for saving life
at sea—he shot the cook. What a trip—we had a cabin for three
—two acrobats and a deformed midget—my wife and I had a
bunk: the ceiling was so low, I had to get out of bed to turn over:
that bunk was more effective than the Pill.

Then they told us on the Tannoy that tomorrow at mid-day we
would cross the Equator—that night we hit an iceberg—and
sunk it. There was a lot of panic with the Captain dashing about
the deck shouting 'Women and children first'—in a gold lamé
dress: I laughed so much I dropped my handbag. I said to him,
'There's a man out there on a raft waving a shirt.' He said:
'Really—what size neck?'

But there's one thing about being on a boat—when you wake up
in the morning—you're not only glad to be alive—but surprised!"

Spike was writing brilliantly and we were going great guns,
then I decided to rest the TV appearances and went back to work
I was not mad about—the clubs. They paid well but artistically it
was not rewarding. The customers are lovely people but by the
time they let you on to do the cabaret spot, which is usually about

eleven pm, their brains are dulled by drink. Spike Mullins' lovely scripts were way over their heads, I could get more applause singing a chorus of "Hands" or "Tulips from Amsterdam" than I could from reciting the words Spike and myself had sweated over to make into good comedy routines.

I was completely bored by most of the work I was doing—very unlike me because usually I love the work I do. I was going to obscurely named places where I knew nobody, places like Greaseboro, Batley, and I was "in Sheffield" for a month one weekend.

If it rained and I couldn't go on the golf course, I twiddled my thumbs in some hotel room. Bob can always find a drinking partner but I get "heady" from drink. What's more, if you don't feel on top of the world it's almost impossible to sing. So I played these dates and apart from one or two, hated every minute of it.

Then something happened quite by accident that made me take off in a career that I hadn't given much thought to—it happened like this.

In November 1970 it was my mother's birthday so I drove over to her house in Welling. The house was very quiet which was most unusual because she loves music; she always has the radio or record player on. I asked her if the radio was broken. She replied, "No, I can't stand all this bomp bomp!" It was all twanging guitars and words she couldn't understand.

I thought what a nice idea it would be to make her a record of all the songs she liked, her own private record with songs like "Me and My Shadow", "Won't you come home, Bill Bailey", "Apple Blossom Time", and "Bye, Bye, Blackbird".

I told Cyril Stapleton who was a recording manager with Pye Records that I'd like to do something like this and his reply was that there must be a lot of people like my mother who would like a list of songs sung similar to the ones I had mentioned. We made the record with a small rhythm group, plus the Tony Mansell Singers and it sounded good when we had it completed. We thought with a bit of luck it might sell five or six thousand copies.

But it didn't—it was quite a failure. Then one day I heard that it was going great guns in Australia, people out there were buying the album by the thousands.

In the middle of one of my TV programmes, Geoff Love interrupted me with the news that I had been awarded a Gold Disc by Astor Records in Australia—it had been flown in by Quantas and he had been asked to present it to me. The audience applauded and

I said to Geoff: "I don't know what to say?" He said: "Don't say anything—sing something from it."

Bob Dixon went into a four bar opening, I sang "Me and My Shadow", then "Moonlight and Roses", into "You were meant for me" and we finished on "You are my Sunshine" with the entire audience joining in. The ovation was unbelievable.

Next day Pye were getting calls from all over Britain from record stores asking for the "Singalong with Max" songs. Pye started pressing for all they were worth, so great was the demand. I was awarded a Gold Disc in just four weeks of the album getting out.

I made another, then another. I have made nine albums in the last two years and every one has got me a Gold or Silver Disc. I am at present working on another volume and all these successes have helped make Pye Records a very valuable company, all from "Singalongamax"—a phrase coined by Cyril Stapleton.

Torquay was too far to visit so I sold the house we had bought there and purchased another at Bournemouth on the West Cliff. It is a big house with panoramic views from the Isle of Wight to Sandbanks. It is my joy. I try to spend every leisure hour I can there. It is under two hours from London.

After a couple of years the kids wandered off again. Anthony now lives in Earls Court. Christine and her family live at Brighton. I sold the house at Leatherhead and moved into London. I have a flat in Victoria. I can be in the dressing room of the Victoria Palace, where I seem to have made my place of work lately, in two minutes —Maxine lives just down the corridor in the same block.

Most weekends we meet at the flat in London or all go down to Bournemouth. Blossom usually does roast beef and we take several hours, drinking wine and chin-wagging.

I must tell you my last story before I wrap this epistle up.

Last summer the entire family were at Bournemouth. I had got this thing about kite flying. It is a great hobby: the feeling is wonderful, holding the twine and feeling the kite tugging up there in the breeze.

The breeze is always good in our garden on the cliff. On this particular evening, I was flying a kite for Michael John—my grandson. Blossom appeared and called me for dinner. I gave the string to Michael who had already eaten and told him to keep it up for me while I had dinner.

I finished dinner. It was dusk so I decided to get the kite in. The breeze had dropped and the kite had dropped about twelve feet down the cliff face. It is a sheer drop of about eighty feet but I thought I could get a rope, fasten it round one of the trees in our garden then go down and retrieve the kite—which cost 29p.

I took a clothes line down that Blossom uses for drying tea towels, which was made of plastic. I threw it over a branch and swung on it, testing to see if it would hold my weight. It was very strong and stood up to the test easily.

I put it round the tree tunk then, showing off to Michael John, I showed him how Alpine climbers do it, with the rope around my chest, under my crotch and round my shoulders, I descended easily. I reached out for the kite and tied it to the rope, then I tried to ascend.

I couldn't make any progress because my hands were perspiring and slipping on the plastic covering of the rope. I tried and could make no progress. I began to worry about my toe hold in the soft cliff face: as I eased my weight on the rope it began to crumble.

Michael up above was getting impatient: "Hurry up, Gramps," he kept shouting. I tried to tell him I wouldn't be long but I knew that I needed help to get back. There was no way I was going to do it. I could feel my fingers swelling as the rope bit in. I had about seventy feet to drop—smack on to the promenade. It was now dark and nobody knew I was there except Michael. I kept slipping an inch or two.

I looked down at the rope and saw I had about six feet to go if my toes didn't hold, I was certain to crash down.

"Michael!" I called, there was no answer, he had got fed up with me playing by myself and gone into the house. "Michael!" I yelled but it was the rowing boat in Hawaii all over again.

Suddenly I heard Bloss calling me: "Max," she said from the top, "what are you playing about at?" In the fading light, she saw me hanging down the cliff. "Oh my God!" she rushed into the house and got Anthony, Barry and Christine, they came out and saw me over the cliff but were helpless.

Blossom rushed in and phoned the fire station. I hung there trying to figure out how I could break the least bones, when I fell —whether it would be better to turn round and crash down on my back or stay as I was and crash down on my face.

With only about two more feet to go on the rope, the fire brigade arrived. One of the firemen looked over the top and shouted: "Hang on, Max—I wanna tell you a story!" Then he laughed his head off. I thought, "Christ, I'm at the end of my tether and he's making jokes." Another fireman with a big thick rope started singing "You Need Hands". It sounded like a script from a Morecambe and Wise Show.

I reached out for the thick rope and was hoisted to safety. When I got back to the house there were ten firemen and eight policemen. The policemen were there because somebody had phoned to say Max Bygraves was committing suicide on the West Cliff.

I walked trembling into the lounge and sipped a large brandy somebody had given me. Then Blossom, with an admonishing finger, said: "That's the last time you play with that kite!"

> Was it really so long?
> Where have all the years gone?
> Where are my young man's days?

PART II

As I approached my fiftieth birthday, which was three years ago, I began to dream of giving showbiz a miss for a while, then find a tropical island where I could sit and write a book, stopping now and then to sip a Campari with soda and to work out the next episode, slowly doing the breast stroke in some crystal clear lagoon.

I then went into a new show at the Victoria Palace, which ran for more than a year—when that finished, I toured harder than I did when I was beginning, this was at home and abroad. After a year of that, I did *another* show back at the Victoria Palace for *another* twelve months.

During the last few weeks of that run, the thoughts of the desert island became more vivid—well, to cut a long story sideways— here I am on a desert island.

Now and then, I finish up with strangers at some cocktail party. Those who have seen me "on the box", or in a show, invariably ask: "What was so and so like?"

As this seems to be a most interesting topic, I have put a few remembrances down on the following pages, they are not meant to be character studies, they are merely there as thoughts I had while doing the breast stroke.

The Bahamas,
January, 1976

MAX MILLER

He was a friendly fellow who thought nothing of helping himself to one of your best jokes. Most every other comedian was lifting Max's gags so he must have figured that it was all right for him to do the same. I can remember telling a joke about a man who walked into a greengrocer's to buy some potatoes. The greengrocer said: "Will you take King Edwards?" The chap said: "No —let him get his own."

In those days, it was a fairly new joke—the following week Max Miller did it on John Sharman's Music Hall radio show. He got a yell with it and I had to cut it out of my act because the whole country had heard it by then.

It was fascinating to watch Max's technique. Before he came on, he got the electrician to black out the stage for about ten seconds, the music would cut off, then quietness came over the auditorium and people were wondering why the show had stopped. The band would suddenly play his signature tune, *Mary from the Dairy*, the lights would go to "full up", the spotlight would hit the "prompt" corner, then at the right moment, on would walk M.M. grinning from ear to ear.

His costume was a flowered dressing-gown, plus-fours that showed multi-coloured socks and a white Anthony Eden hat set at 45°, already the audience was laughing helplessly. He would then remove the dressing-gown to show a bright yellow suit. His back cloth was invariably a street scene with a lamp-post.

He would walk to the lamp-post and hang the dressing-gown on the bar just below the light. The music would still be playing, he would then walk down stage and flicker his eyelashes, he was heavily made up by today's standards, with a lot of mascara and eye-liner on the eyes.

Up till now he hadn't spoken a word—he was doing what most comedians try all their lives for, to "get" an audience in the first ten seconds of their entrance. Now, with the whole theatre laughing at the loudness of the yellow suit, he'd speak: "D'ye like it, lady? I've just had a mustard bath!" He would say this over the music, the music would cut off on that joke and the hundreds of customers suddenly heard the volume of their own laughter. It was magic to watch. There was nobody to touch him.

When in London, he insisted on going on the bill early during the second house, to enable him to get home to Brighton—in those days, the last train left Victoria at eleven pm. He was very close with his money and could see no sense in paying for a season ticket and not using it.

He never tipped stage hands—I asked him once if it was true about not giving the stage staff gratuities, he was amazed: "What for?" His eyebrows went up to the widow's peak of his toupe. "They don't do anything for me—they drop my cloth in from the flies—then they sod off into the pub for a quarter of an hour while I'm performing—tip 'em!—if it wasn't for me, they wouldn't bloody well be working!"

That was how he got his name for meanness, but I am assured by quite a lot of people who know that he was charitable in many other ways.

When the BBC were doing *This is Your Life*, I was the subject for one of the programmes. Max Miller came on, he talked about how he admired me, which you really have to do on that sort of programme, but made his exit with one of the biggest laughs in the programme when he said: "Don't forget, son—always work hard —change your material—and never—*never*—tell blue jokes."

Soon after that, he was dead from a heart attack, but he had the best years of the variety world. I am not so sure he would have survived in the television era. I may be wrong, but Max needed the freedom of a stage and an audience that was *not* permissive, *he* was the permissive one, or so he led us to believe. I somehow think the balance would have been against him in today's world of so-called freedom.

JUDY GARLAND

If I had the wit, the wisdom and the learning of one of my favourite authors, J. B. Priestley, I could probably paint a much better picture in words of this colourful character who was born in 1922 with the unlikely name of Frances Gumm.

She toured with her two sisters, who also had the unlikely name of the Gumm Sisters, a singing act. The story goes that she was discovered for Hollywood by MGM producer Joe Pasternak.

It was policy to have a crowd of children on the payrolls in those days, children were big box office. Ever since Jackie Coogan walked with Charlie Chaplin, there had been a conveyor belt full of them: Shirley Temple, Mickey Rooney, Jane Withers, Jackie Cooper, the Dead End Kids and, of course, Frances Gumm, who had her name changed to Judy Garland.

I first met her in the stalls of the London Palladium early one Monday morning in 1951; she was a lot plumper than I had seen or imagined her in real life. I think it was her very first time in England and like most people in a foreign land was eager to be friendly. She shook hands with everybody, plus a cheerful "Hi!"

and that dazzling Garland smile we had seen so many times in close-up on the enormous screens at the ABC or the Ritz cinemas.

We all warmed to her right away. We watched her rehearse an act that was very different to the act she did shortly afterwards. At that time, she was not very solvent so her entourage consisted of her pianist and manager, Sid Luft.

The act was mediocre because of its simplicity. She had not been earning from films which had been her living for the past few years, she couldn't even get a night-club booking of any standing in the USA, so she arrived at the Palladium with a singing act that included all her hits: *Over the Rainbow, The Trolley Song, We're a Couple of Swells, The Boy Next Door, Swanee* and *Get Happy*. Most of these, with a couple of special material numbers that included a song about how nice it was to be in London, took about twenty-five minutes. That's all Val Parnell wanted because there were two houses nightly at the Palladium. Somehow they got two thousand five hundred people out of the first house, swept and cleaned the place, then got the same number in again, all in twelve minutes.

I have had to smile at various writings I have read about Judy Garland, and at people outside the theatre world who tut-tut and say: "That poor girl!" That poor girl lived every moment of every day. I worked side by side with her for well over a year and not on one day did I ever see her down in the mouth. She had a God-given talent that she rarely stinted on once in front of an audience. What she couldn't stand was the boredom, the waiting to go on stage, but once out there, she enjoyed every moment.

The act she did in New York was a lot different to the one in London. Eight dancing boys were brought from Hollywood to build up the act. Roger Edens wrote special material and "Chuck" Walters arrived from Los Angeles to produce it.

After New York went wild in its acclamation of her, the parties started—from midnight till dawn, the chorus boys brought their "friends". Anybody who was anybody wanted Judy at their party. All and sundry told her how great she was; you've got to start believing it, if it is said as often as it was said to her.

Sure she drank, but she enjoyed it and if there had been a theatre she could have gone to every evening, she'd have enjoyed it till this day, I'm sure. It's that terrible boredom. She didn't know how to read a book, or crochet, or knit a sweater. Beware of that boredom, I tell most people in our business. Play golf, or study butterflies, or read or write, anything so long as you are occupied.

Judy Garland was one of my favourite people. When I read of her death at such an early age, I was saddened but not surprised.

TED RAY

Ted Ray has a mind with a filing index built in. If he had to speak at a surgeon's dinner, he would produce fifteen minutes that would have those members of the medical world helpless with laughter. He could do the same for footballers, for actors or for politicians. He could have the literary profession in stitches because he is well-read. He has this insatiable desire for knowledge.

I have known him over twenty years—each time we have met he has had a new story or anecdote. He was a guest on my television show on two different occasions and for the week we rehearsed he had stagehands, electricians, cast and production staff listening to the stories he would deliver with eyebrows raised, never seeming to come down till the pay-off of the joke. Then he would laugh as much as his audience.

I think he is proud of this filing cabinet that he calls a brain. It is impossible to tell him a new joke without him saying, "That reminds me . . ." He doesn't do it to be funnier or because he wants to top you, it is because you have pushed a button in that system that reminds him of joke 78, or joke 7312.

To illustrate this, I tell of the last time I saw him which, at the time of writing, was only a few weeks ago. He was in a bad way, a patient in the North Middlesex Hospital, very badly injured from a motoring accident. He had bones broken all over his body and it was almost impossible for him to move. He was delighted to see me. I stayed for almost three hours. I would have stayed longer but he was getting tired. Before I left, he told me an unbelievable story . . . I will try to tell it the way he told it to me lying there in that private ward.

"Max—the only connection with the nurse and the outside world is this bell-push." He held up a pear-shaped bell-push with a white plunger that was supposed to alarm the nurse if he should need assistance. "If that goes, I am alone . . . Well, this morning at three am, I needed a bedpan . . . I pushed the bell and I knew that it wasn't working—the spring had gone on the plunger . . . I called but it was no use . . . I was panic-stricken . . . I didn't want to disgrace myself so I decided to do something . . . I pulled the bed-

clothes back and managed to get my feet on the floor . . . it seemed
to take a lifetime . . . I made my way across the room and, see that
plant in that pot?" He pointed to a large pot with a plant in, sent
from a well-wisher. "I took the plant out and managed to put the
pot on the floor . . . I then undid my pyjamas and managed to sit
on the pot . . . Just as I did so, the light went on . . . in walked
Eamonn Andrews and said: 'Ted Ray—This is Your Life!'"

He actually had me believing it. He had used me as an audience
to see if his wit was as sharp as it was before the accident.

He's still in a bad way but recovering. I am glad he is because
whenever Ted Ray walks into your life, he seems to leave quite a
lot of sunshine behind.

DAME EDITH EVANS

When Edith Evans "breezed" into the rehearsal room, she was
seventy-six, she was followed by four or five people all ready to
catch her in case she disintegrated. "Hello," she said, smiling and
fluttering her eyelids, "what a pleasure it is to be working with *you*."

We were about to rehearse a number for a charity show at the
London Palladium, it was the song that Maurice Chevalier had
duetted with Hermione Gingold in the film *Gigi*—the song *I
Remember It Well*—would be the first time in a very long career
that Edith Evans had *ever* sung on a stage.

The pleasure, of course, was all mine; I had admired her performances over a long period and to be doing a number with this
well-loved actress filled me with pride.

We spent a lot of time rehearsing it—it was produced by William
Chappel, whose idea it was in the first place to team us together on
what was a star-studded bill.

When I say, in all modesty, that our offering was the hit of the
night this can be judged by the seven or eight curtain calls we took
to a delighted audience—of course, it was mostly for Dame Edith
who, using that beautiful instrument she calls a voice, blended with
a string orchestra, cast a magic spell over the "standing-room-only"
auditorium.

I thought she would be retiring soon after that but, lo and
behold, ten years later, well into her eighties, she turned up on the
Parkinson TV show. She was bright-eyed, articulate and *very* funny.
As I watched, I found myself wondering whether we could repeat

the song we had done a decade earlier. I had a TV series at that moment and was on the look-out for "unusual" guests. I decided to call her agent and invite her on my show to do the *I Remember It Well* number. She was delighted I had asked, and accepted.

She arrived at the ATV studios in Elstree after travelling from Kent in her Rolls Royce—she had decided not to drive herself so had a friend do it for her.

We had sent her a script with a little humour in, well, we thought it was humorous—it had been written by Eric Davidson, one of our best television comedy writers, and the premise was that Dame Edith could never get my name right—she would call me Mr Hargreaves—Max Bywaters—Max Seagrave—anything but my right name of Bygraves.

Almost as she entered the room, she waved the script at the entire ensemble and said, "I can't do this—it's all wrong!"

"What is wrong with it, Dame Edith?" I asked.

"Calling you Hargreaves—everybody knows you are Bygraves."

"But that is the joke," I tried to explain.

"Well, it isn't funny—not to me, anyway—it is degrading you— you have worked years to establish your name, to ridicule you like that is, well—er—it's rude!" She looked down her nose at the scriptwriter. "I suggest we change it!" That was final.

It was like the headmistress had reprimanded us all. "All right," muttered Davidson. "Okay," said the director, not daring to argue. "We'll come up with something else," I promised.

We didn't come up with anything else, we were all too afraid to venture any suggestions for humour—we all knew we were on the wrong wavelength. We settled for just saying, "Good evening," to each other. I admired her dress, she said: "Thank you." We went into the song and it made a perfect three or four minutes of television. Next day, friends, taxi-drivers, road sweepers and waiters, stopped me to say how wonderful they thought we were together. I cannot think of anything I have done that impressed an audience more.

Shortly afterwards, I went to see her one-woman show at the Haymarket Theatre—I thrilled to her "know-how", laughed at her quips and applauded the mastery of her craft.

After the show, I took my wife back-stage to meet her—she was delighted to see us and made us very welcome. Some friends of hers arrived shortly after and she gushed to them, "I want you to meet one of my favourite men." She took my arm and announced: "Here he is . . . Max Bywaters!"

Jack went to a great deal of trouble to impress upon people that he was mean—he went to more trouble to convince them that he was even more generous.

I first met him at a party in New York twenty-five years ago. We became friends and kept in touch right to the end of his life.

A few weeks after we met, he gave me an eighteen-carat gold money clip engraved "From Jack—to Max". I have it to this day. It amuses people that the mean Jack Benny would give away a money clip.

Comedians, more than anybody, are accused of meanness. Max Miller was thought to be very close with a shilling. There are acquaintances of Arthur Askey who swear they have never seen him put his hand in his pocket and buy a drink. I have been branded with the same disease, yet somehow, I seem to get through thousands of pounds each year that have my accountant tut-tutting and waving an admonishing finger.

Jack had to tip twice as much as anybody else when he left a restaurant or paid a cab-driver. He did it to save face. He couldn't bear to think of anybody thinking bad of him.

He was a great fan of mine. Early last year, the BBC's Radio 2 did a four-week serial on my life. Different people spoke about my career. One of these was Jack Benny. He said that he saw a lot of himself in me, although we didn't work in the same way, and he told of how impressed he was when he saw me in the Judy Garland Show at the New York Palace.

He liked the way I constructed an idea and then milked it to extract all the laughs possible from it. I was one of the first comedians to go to America in the post World War II years and he noted how I had adapted my material for the USA.

Everything he said made me feel ten feet tall because there is nothing we on the other side of the footlights like to hear more than genuine praise. It makes the blood flow freer and it also makes it easier to sleep.

Jack felt safe on radio and later on television. What scared him to the end of his days were night-club audiences. His act needed rapt attention—therefore, waiters that served while he was performing unnerved him and the thought of hecklers petrified him. His act was one "long take". Anything else moving would be distraction. He would always have several writers on hand to re-write material that wasn't "going over".

If a writer gave him a gem of a line he would tell everybody what a fine line and what a fine writer the creator was.

His agent, Irving Fein, once booked him for a dinner at a club in Los Angeles, just several blocks from where he lived. By the time Jack got on, most of the audience were full of "lunatic broth". But they settled down for Jack's act. All except one very drunken man who decided to heckle him.

Jack fought a losing battle with the lush. He was never a master of the ad lib and the drunk was getting more laughs than he was.

Eventually, Jack decided the only way to stop him was to put his cards on the table. As nicely as he knew how, Jack said, "Listen, friend—you may not like me—but there are quite a lot of people here who have paid good money to hear what I have to say—please let me do the job I'm paid for and let me entertain these folk—if you want to heckle, do it after I've done my job of work." The audience applauded this logic and shushed the inebriated one. Jack proceeded with his act but confided to me it wasn't as good as it should have been because he had one eye on the drunk, conse-quently, his timing was suffering.

It came to the part of the act where he produces his violin. As he put it to his chin, he said in that droll Benny delivery, "This, ladies and gentlemen, is a Stradivarius—it was made in 1781 . . ."

The drunk, who had been very quiet since Jack had asked him to be, suddenly came to life on the line about Stradivarius making it in 1781 and yelled: "Did you buy it new?"

The whole place fell about laughing and Jack walked over to the sozzler and shook his hand. He confessed that if he'd lived to be a thousand, he would never have thought of a line comparable to that one.

Jack would repeat himself on stories which is usually the first thing a comedian learns *not* to do. It is important you remember who you told the story to. Nothing lets you down more than telling a story to the same audience. You must train yourself not to do this, otherwise people realise you are not as spontaneous as you pretend.

In the later years of his life, he would go over anecdotes you had heard maybe four or five times. Always told equally well but losing something because of their familiarity.

In one of the last concerts I saw him do, which was only a short time before his death at eighty years of age, I watched him on the stage of the Palladium tell the same joke twice. His comic instinct told him by the laugh that didn't come, that he had made a faux pas. "Did I tell that joke earlier?" he asked the audience. There was a mumbled "yes" to his question.

"Good," he said, "I just wanted to see if you were paying attention!"

He made Americans laugh for close on fifty years. It would be hard to find a better epitaph than that.

SIR ALEC GUINNESS

I was once asked to be Master of Ceremonies at a Royal Film Première. The film shown was *The Horse's Mouth*, it starred Alec Guinness. The film didn't set the world on fire but it was a modest success. The audience was filled with personalities and after the show we were invited by the distributors to have dinner at the Mayfair Hotel.

It turned out to be one of the most miserable affairs I have ever been to. It was arranged for a personality to sit at a table of eight or ten people who were the wives and relatives of the Wardour Street office—there were friends of the cameramen, director, all foreigners to people like Peter Finch, Terry-Thomas, Peter Sellers and Alec Guinness, who were there to boost the publicity for the film.

Pete Sellers and myself managed to meet in the gents' toilet and confided to each other what a bloody awful time we were having. "Can't we liven it up, somehow?" he asked.

He knew I played the piano a little. As we walked back into the ballroom, the band had taken a break. Peter said: "Come on, Max —let's have a go!" He sat at the drums (he is a very good drummer), I sat at the piano and we had a little fun, back came the bass player and clarinettist to a small ripple of applause, and slowly the party began to swing.

Couples began to dance, the pianist took his seat, I began to vocalise—and from something that had been dead minutes before, the room started jumping, as they say.

I told a couple of jokes and before you could say "I'm a ham!" personalities were queuing up to do their party piece at the microphone. Terry-Thomas did a routine, Peter Sellers did some impressions, Peter Finch told a filthy story about an actor "pissing" from the balcony of a theatre, which made every lady and some of the gentlemen blush, then amidst all this, without being asked, Alec Guinness made his way towards the microphone.

This quiet man who we had to strain to listen to, suddenly announced he would give his impression of a man on a train going to the toilet. After Peter Finch's episode, we were a bit worried because strangely enough, I have seen many straight actors try to be funny and all they really do is finish up being terribly coarse— they tell the sort of stories that should be kept for Green Rooms or stag parties.

However, Alec's contribution was of a man sitting on a train holding a newspaper reading it, all the time he does the mime he makes a "yakkity-yak" noise quietly to give the impression of the train roaring along; he opens the carriage door, still going "yakkity-yak" several times louder, it is a very funny piece of business and he finished to loud applause. He bowed and went back to his table.

It is the only time I met him—next day, he wrote me a letter thanking me for my help in making the evening go with a swing.

I enjoy him—I adore his work—but isn't it awful—I can never look at him without thinking of a toilet.

MILTON SHULMAN

I am a believer in righting injustices. A few weeks ago, I wrote to a well-known columnist who had announced, unbelievingly, that *he* was fed up with Richard Burton and Elizabeth Taylor; they had become bores, he said, then, as if he was the guardian of the public he pretends to be, he let it be known that from now on there would be no more references in *his* column to the Burtons who, as he said, were bores.

I read it and thought what a bloody cheek the fellow has. I wrote to say that if Burton and Taylor are the bores he says they are, it is because people like him have made them so. I don't suppose they would care an iota if the media didn't print another word or take another picture, if their private lives were left a little more private.

I once opened the *Sunday Express* and read in the John Gordon column a reference to Elizabeth Taylor, which began: "This ageing old bag . . ." Well! No gentleman should ever use that sort of approach to a lady. I wrote and told him so. I got a letter back from the editor saying that John Gordon had died on the very day I sent the letter. I wrote back to say that dying was no excuse. I didn't get a reply.

The first time I met Milton Shulman, who is a very good journalist and critic, was at a party given to honour Charlie Chaplin at the Savoy Hotel. I was speaking to him for ten minutes before I found out he was Milton Shulman.

Most of us in the theatre business worry about this fellow. The only reason I mention him in this book is because he is one of the very few critics who can sum up an act or play and tell them where it has gone wrong, but—and this is a big "but"—he also manages in most cases to suggest how to put it right or suggest an alternative. He won't be too harsh on beginners but will come down on anything too shoddy.

He has sometimes been hard and sometimes glowing about me but always fair, even if I laid an egg with an audience or died on my feet, he has always let me know that "dying is no excuse". I've got a lot of time for Mr Shulman, he has given me a lot of informative pleasure over the years.

FRANKIE HOWERD

Frank, as I call him, is a complex. I know we are all put on this earth to be different, but he is "way out".

We met in 1946, when we were both fresh out of the armed forces—me out of the RAF, him out of the army. Neither of us had risen to any dizzy heights—he got to lance corporal, me to LAC, this, after almost five years' service.

We were thrown together in a revue called *For the fun of it*. Almost every week in another town, we shared a dressing-room—for months and months, the show ran and as I got to know him more and more, I seemed to know him less and less.

I never truthfully thought that he would be a star comedian. His act was built on its amateurishness, he was a droll who could go, say from Newcastle where we'd be appearing, and "tear them up", then go a few miles further on to Sunderland where he would flop miserably. On a particular Saturday night as I stood in the wings watching him struggle with the audience, I heard a crack like a pistol had been fired. After the show, the stage manager found a rivet, the type used for ship building, that someone had thrown from the gallery. If it had hit him, it could have done him great harm. He never forgot Sunderland.

He was gangling even then. We were about the same size, I had just had a suit made during the run of the show and it fitted me like a glove. Frank asked me if he could purchase it from me; suits were hard to come by in those days, as clothing coupons were required. I let him have it for what I had paid for it. He tried it on and looked as good as it is possible for *him* to look in a suit. Several days later he came into the room with the suit in a bag, he put it on the back of a chair—not a hanger, he was an untidy man. "Where have you been with the suit?" I asked. He told me he had had a few alterations made by a local tailor.

When he walked on the stage in the suit, I saw he'd had the sleeves shortened by a couple of inches, because, he said; "I work with my wrists." I couldn't believe a performer could have had a perfectly good suit ruined to show an audience his wrists. His act was made up mostly of several choruses of *Three Little Fishes*, the ones that swam and swam all over the dam—as he demonstrated the fish swimming, he needed the wrists to demonstrate.

He had a great way (still has) of appearing to be helpless and so getting you running around for him. You'd find yourself going to the chemist to get his razor blades, his shaving soap, his meat ration, fixing his digs for the following week. All this you'd do because somewhere in his make-up you'd sense greatness, it seemed you were honoured to run these errands for him, it didn't occur to you that he was "using" you.

But it didn't worry any of us too much if we marched off to the shops to do his chores while he slept at the digs. We thought he was creating.

In J. B. Priestley's book, he suggests that Frank didn't need funny material, that he *is* a funny man; I don't agree with J.B. on this. Frank needed material more than any of us, he was getting through too much with his regular broadcasting that came after he "made it" in 1948. This, after only two short years as a professional.

One of the best things that happened to him as far as funny material went, was Eric Sykes. He wrote some of his funniest routines, then, later on, Alan Simpson with Ray Galton.

When the public became "conditioned" to Frank through the medium of radio, he was a sensation. Never have I heard the volume of laughter engineered by a single performer before or since, his begging them to "No—listen! Listen to Francis!" made the theatres rock from Plymouth to Glasgow.

Like all performers with so much going for them, the "ups" are followed by the "downs". These periods made him morose and run away from it all—in those days, he hadn't figured out how to pace it, nowadays maturity has made him accept the ups and downs together.

He was badly handled and really didn't get the deserts he should have got from a sparkling career.

The last time I spoke to him was on the phone in Australia two years ago—he had notched up another great success in his TV series *Up Pompeii*! He had gone to Australia to garner some of the profit to be made from personal appearances there.

I don't worry about Frank. He is a friend I would do anything for if he needed me, but he doesn't need me. I'll bet at this very moment wherever he is, he has somebody getting his razor blades, his shaving soap, his meat ration, etc., etc.

GARY COOPER

I only met him for a brief moment. It was in the gentleman's cloakroom at the Dorchester Hotel. As I stood gazing at the glazing, I casually looked at my neighbour, who was doing the same as me.

It was a most familiar face. "Aren't you—er—" I stammered. He said, "Yep." Then zipped his fly, washed his hands and was gone.

HENRY COOPER

Almost everybody warms to Henry. He is a lovable man who can get as many laughs as any of the comedians around today.

I like being on a bill with Henry—I like to follow him—he makes me sound educated.

It is hard to believe that this gentle person was only a step or two away from proving himself the world's most invincible heavyweight. I have known a lot of boxers, but apart from Henry, Dave Charnley and Tommy Farr, I cannot think of any others in Great

Britain who have managed to leave the game with a few quid behind them.

As long as Henry can talk, he will always be in demand. We were recently doing a charity show for the handicapped up at Turnberry in Scotland. The "do" was to raise as much as we could to buy ambulances. Several well-known acts did a "turn" and the audience was ecstatic.

It came to Henry's turn to tell a few stories and he was trembling with fear, he had never done his party piece in front of a lot of Scots before, but he did fantastically well, and finished to a standing ovation. I was so pleased for him, I could have kissed him, but you don't go around kissing heavyweight champions in public.

It came to my turn and I must confess I was apprehensive because I had to "close" the bill—it meant following an hour of superb entertainment, but I managed to pull a few tricks I had remembered from working in Scotland several years previously and finished winning.

I did four encores—when I eventually sat down at the table, Henry, so pleased for me, jumped up, put his arms round me and *kissed* me! He is now known in our circle as Henry the Poof!

You may be happy to hear that from those wonderful Scots we raised £21,000—not bad for one day's effort!

CHARLIE DRAKE

I used to play a lot of golf with Charlie, but packed it up when I kept losing him under divots.

ERIC SYKES

If I was ever asked to write a piece for *Reader's Digest*—the one entitled: "My most unforgettable character"—I would choose Eric.

This man has surmounted more than any performer I know of.

He wandered into show business as a writer for Frankie Howerd. He left his home town of Oldham and set out for London shortly after the war to become a script writer, a dangerous way of making a living in those days because we didn't use writers. All our jokes came from books, magazines and "borrowing" from other comedians. If we paid £5 for a page of jokes, we hoped they would last us for the next two or three years, but from writing for people like Howerd, myself and a couple of others, Eric managed to survive in a garret somewhere in the Earls Court Road.

His big chance came when he wrote *Educating Archie*—an award-winning radio show—from that, he became solvent but lacked the business brain he has acquired lately.

Most of his time was spent beating the clock. He drank more than he should have done, he didn't eat regularly, he neglected himself and soon his thin frame was in a hospital bed where he met a pretty nurse named Edith, who he married.

It was lucky he did, because she nursed him back to health. During the time he was ill, he lost contact with the hit writing he had been churning out—writers had their own comedians and comedy show.

It was then he decided to act out his own writing. With a team that consisted of Hattie Jacques, Richard Wattis and Derek Guyler, he now has the honour of appearing in the longest running television series in the world, twenty years to be exact.

We have travelled world wide together, slept in dumps and the finest hotel rooms, covered thousands of miles as car companions and never had a cross word with each other.

I despair with him. He should be one of the richest men in our business but through the years he has picked bad advisers, bad investments and impossible dreams.

Only recently, he put all his money into a film project that is half finished, he cannot raise the money to come up with the finished article.

What is so commendable is that he backs himself to the hilt, never begs or borrows. All this against an affliction of deafness that would have left most men helpless.

He is a lovely man, so proud, so honest but so bloody gullible it makes you want to cry.

One day I will try to write a book about him.

I must go for another swim.

Index

Abbot and Costello, 91
Adams, Granny, 25
Adler, Ernest, 99
Adrienne, Jean, 86
Aku, 137, 139
Alexandra, Princess, 161
Alhambra, Glasgow, 146
Allen, Gracie, 106
Ambrose, 36
Andrews, Eamonn, 180
Andrews, Julie, 96, 97, 102, 112
Arnold, Tom, 101, 111
Askey, Arthur, 182
Atlas, Charles, 39
Atwell, Winifred, 111–12, 115, 116

Baker, Hylda, 111
Bakewell, Joan, 108
Barclay, Jack, 112
Barnes, Brian, 153, 154
BBC, 85, 86, 94, 165
Beatles, 107, 136, 163
Beery, Wallace, 46
Bennett, Billy, 43
Benny, Jack, 106–107, 108, 182–4
Bernard Brothers, 111
Bernstein, Lord, 164, 165
Bless 'em all, 89
Bloom, John, 119
Bricusse, Leslie, 114, 126
Brough, Peter, 96, 101–102
Burns, George, 106
Burton, Richard, 185
Bushell, David, 123–4
Butlin, Billy, 164, 165
Bygraves, Anthony, 88, 98, 103, 104, 119–21, 132, 134, 149–52, 162–3, 169, 170
Bygraves, "Blossom", 79–81, 85, 86, 88, 98, 103, 104, 105, 117–21, 126, 127, 132, 133, 134, 155, 156, 158–9, 169, 170, 171
Bygraves, Christine, 80, 86, 88, 98, 103, 126, 127–8, 131–2, 133, 152, 163, 169, 170
Bygraves, Grandfather, 29, 67
Bygraves, Harry, 14, 21, 25–6, 29, 30, 36, 39–40, 60, 62, 67, 110–11, 156
Bygraves, Lil, 14, 29, 67, 156
Bygraves, Max, parents and family life, 13–14, 54–5, 59–60, 67–8, 109–111; school, 14, 15, 51–3; and street sellers, 16–17; thieving, 21–23; Mosley Rally, 23–4; childhood "Holidays", 24, 25–6; singing at parties, 29; shoe repairing, 30–1; cinema-going, 35; listening to the radio, 35–6; and a "flasher", 36–37; fighting, 37–9; first "appearance" on stage, 45–7; sings in Westminster Cathedral, 51–3; convalescence in Ramsgate, 53–5; on teachers, 55–6; goes for page boy's job, 56–8; first job, 58–9, 61–2, 71; building jobs, 71–2; joins the RAF, 72, 75–9; gets married, 79–81; entertainment and the RAF, 81–2; demob and BBC work, 85–6; *For the fun of it*, 86–7, birth of Anthony and home of his own, 88–9; signs with Jock Jacobsen, 89–90; at the London Palladium, 91, 94, 97–8, 111, 112, 113–115, 131; Royal Variety Performances, 91–4, 115–16, 143; and *Educating Archie*, 94, 96–7, 98, 101–102; birth of Maxine, 95–6; appears with Judy Garland, 97–8, 99–101, 103, 107, 109, 177–8;

Bygraves, Max—*contd.*
    records, 97, 168–9; Friern Barnet
    house, 98–9; in Hollywood, 103–
    107; on American TV, 107–109;
    buys first Rolls, 112; and Alassio,
    113, 125–6; *We're having a ball*,
    114, 121; "investments", 116–19;
    songwriting, 121; and *A Cry from
    the Streets*, 122–5; new home at
    Oxshott, 126–8; trips to Australia,
    131–6, 155–6; *Do-re-mi*, 131; Ivor
    Novello Award, 121, 136; in
    Hawaii, 136–9; lunch with the
    Queen, 144–6; *Five Past Eight*,
    146; writes for newspapers, 146–9;
    trip to the Far East, 149–52; in
    South Africa, 153–5; holiday in
    Fiji, 156–60; show in Dallas, 160–
    162; "Permissive Society", 163–4;
    television show *Max*, 164–7, 168;
    clubs, 167–8; on Bournemouth
    cliff, 169–71
Bygraves, Maxine, 95–6, 98, 103,
    104, 132, 152, 163, 169
Bygraves, Mrs (Mother), 13, 14, 24,
    29, 36, 40, 45, 60, 62, 67, 75, 110–
    111, 156, 168
Bygraves, Mr (Father), 13, 14, 21,
    22–3, 24–5, 29, 30, 36, 39–40, 45,
    46, 59, 60, 62–3, 67, 110, 156
Bygraves, Pat, 14, 29, 156

Caen, Herb, 108
Caine, Michael, 36
Campion, Mrs, 40
Cantor, Eddie, 99
Carrol Gibbons Band, 89
Chambers, Paul, 164, 165
Champ, The, 46
Chaplin, Charlie, 46, 177, 186
Chappel, William, 180
Charley Moon, 114
Charnley, Dave, 188
Chasen, Dave, 106
Chelsea Palace, 89
Christmas, Art, 86
Clift, Montgomery, 99
Coconut Grove, 105
Cogan, Alma, 115

Collins, Mr, 38
Como, Perry, 108
Conway, Steve, 89
Coogan, Jackie, 46, 177
Cooper, Gary, 99, 188
Cooper, Henry, 188–9
Cooper, Jackie, 177
Costa, Sam, 89
Cotton, Billy, 111, 112, 113
Country Life, 126
Crawford, Joan, 106
Crawley, Johnny, 38–9
Crosby, Bing, 67, 108
Cry from the Streets, A, 122–4

Daily Herald, 61, 62
Davidson, Eric, 181
Dead End Kids, the, 177
Delfont, Bernard, 119, 164, 165
Depression, the, 30
Dietrich, Marlene, 106
Dixon, Bob, 102, 103, 105, 112, 132,
    133, 136–7, 150, 152–3, 160–1, 162,
    163, 168, 169
Dodd, Ken, 43
Drake, Charlie, 165, 189
Dulay, Peter, 126

Eaton, Shirley, 113
Eden, Anthony, 115
Edens, Roger, 99, 178
Educating Archie, 94, 96–7, 98, 101–
    102, 190
Elizabeth II, 115, 143
Elizabeth, the Queen Mother, 91,
    143
English, Flight Sergeant, 77–8
Evans, Dame Edith, 180–1
Evening News, 147

Farr, Tommy, 188
Fascists, 23–4
Fein, Irving, 183
Fields, Gracie, 43, 115
Financial Times, 117, 119
Finch, Peter, 184, 185
Finsbury Park Empire, 90, 91
Fisher's Wharf, 29
Flanagan, Bud, 115

Fleet Street, 58, 61
Fleming, Ian, 151
Flotsam and Jetsam, 43
For the fun of it, 86–7, 89
Formby, George, 43
Frankau, Ronald, 43
Fyffe, Will, 146

Gable, Clark, 103
Galton, Ray, 187
Garbo, Greta, 35
Gardner, Ava, 104, 105
Garland, Judy, 91, 94, 97–8, 99–101, 103, 107, 109, 177–9
Gaynor, Mitzi, 106
George VI, 91
Gerrard, Tony, 44–7
Getty, Paul, 164, 165
Gilbert, Lewis, 122–3
Gleason, Jackie, 108
Gordon, John, 185–6
Graham, Sheilah, 105–106
Grauman's Chinese Theatre, 103
Green, Barry, 152, 163, 170
Greene, Hughie, 44
Guinness, Sir Alec, 184–5
Guyler, Derek, 190

Hall, Henry, 36
Hancock, Tony, 96, 101–102
Harker, Gordon, 36, 57
Harris, Phil, 106
Harris, Wee Willie, 121
Hay, Will, 36
Hearne, Richard, 112, 113
Henderson, Dickie, 115, 162
Henry, Charles, 98
Hitchcock, Alfred, 106
Holborn Empire, 58–9
Holloway, Stanley, 36
Hollywood Reporter, 105
Horse's Mouth, The, 184
Howerd, Frankie, 85, 86, 87, 90, 121, 186–8, 189, 190
Hurran, Dickie, 146
"Hutch", 43
Hylton, Jack, 119

Investor, 117
ITV, 165

Jacobsen, Jock, 89, 90, 97, 99, 106, 109, 116, 124, 136, 160
James, Jimmy, 88
Jacques, Hattie, 96, 102, 190
John Sharman's Music Hall, 176
Jolson, Al, 89, 100
Jones, Phillip, 166

Kathleen, nanny, 132
Kaye Sisters, 114
Kellino, Pamela, 104
Kennedy, Arthur, 106
Kennedy, John, 153, 161–2
Kid, The, 46
King, Martin Luther, 153
Knight, Ma, 87

La Rue, Danny, 166
Lamour, Dorothy, 91
Landau, Flight Lieutenant, 85
Latin Quarter, 111
Lauder, Harry, 146
Leeman, Dicky, 126
Leslie, Colin, 114
Leslie, Eddie, 86
Levinson, Lou, 112
Levy, Lou, 137
Lewis, Harry, 62–3
Lewis, Jean, 110
Liberace, 115–16
Locke, Bobby, 153–4, 155
London Palladium, 85, 90, 91–4, 104, 110, 111, 177, 178, 180
Love, Geoff, 166, 168
Loy, Myrna, 35
Luft, Sid, 99, 101, 109, 178
Lynn, Vera, 82
Lyon, Ben, 115
Lyon-Shaw, Bill, 87

McCrea, Joel, 35
MacDonald, Aimi, 166
MacDonald, Johnnie, 35
McNally, Nurse, 53–4, 79
Manchester Palace, 94–5
Marks, Alfred, 15
Marlow, Mrs, 21–2, 110
Marx, Groucho, 113–14
Mason, James, 104

Matthews, Jack, 111
Miller, Billy, 105
Miller, Max, 43, 75, 175-7, 182
Minnelli, Liza, 165
Moffett, Graham, 36
Monkhouse, Bob, 115
Monty, Hal, 89
Morecambe and Wise, 165, 171
Moreton, Robert, 96
Morley, Robert, 107, 108
Mosley, Oswald, 23
Moss Empires, 86, 90, 114
Mullins, Spike, 147, 166-8
Murray, Barbara, 122
Murray, Miss, 51-3
Murray, Mrs, 80
Muscroft, Hedley, 153, 154

Neatrour, Andy, 119
Neiman Marcus, 161
New Cross Empire, 43, 44-7
Nicholls, Joy, 111
Nitty Nora, 21
Nitwits, The, 89
Nitwits on Parade, 89
Noble, Peter, 94
Nottingham Empire, 91

O'Connor, Denis, 53, 54
O'Connor, Mr, 52
Ogilvy, Hon. Angus, 161
Olivier, Laurence, 115
Oswald, Lee Harvey, 161

Pangbourne, Franklin, 57
Paramor, Norrie, 82
Parnell, Val, 90, 91, 97, 111, 114, 115, 178
Pasternak, Joe, 177
Payne, Norman, 89
Peers, Donald, 86, 87, 91
Perkins, Billy, 46
Pertwee, Jon, 112
Petticoat Lane, 15, 62-3
Philip, Prince, 143
Ponticelli, Ernest, 87
Powell, Sandy, 29
Powell, William, 35

Priestley, J. B., 177, 187
Pupa, Piccola, 126

Ray, Ted, 90, 179-80
Regan, Joan, 114
Reid, Beryl, 166
Rennie, Drew, 147
Richard, Cliff, 121
Richards, Louise, 132
Richards, Michael, 126, 128, 131, 132, 133
Richards, Michael John, 131, 132, 169, 170
Ridley, Wally, 96-7
Roberts, Alfie, 23
Ronalde, Ronnie, 98
Rooney, Mickey, 177
Rose, Jack, 81

Saint Anne's Youth Club, 95
Saint Joseph's School, 51-3
San Francisco Examiner, 108
Savoy Hotel, 56-8
Scott, Terry, 165
Scottish Daily Express, 146
"Scrag", the Cat's Meat Man, 15-16
Secombe, Harry, 115
Sellers, Peter, 113-14, 184
Seventh Heaven, 80
Sherwood, Tony, 82
Shulman, Milton, 185-6
Simpson, Alan, 187
Sinatra, Frank, 91, 99, 104, 105
Six-five Special, 121
"Skates", the Fish Man, 16
Skimpy in the Navy, 89
Slennet, Ben, 77, 78, 79
"Spot", the dog, 46, 47
Stapleton, Cyril, 168, 169
Steele, Tommy, 121, 124
Stewart, Bill, 166
Stewart, James, 80
Stordahl, Axel, 105
Strange, Rene, 86
Sullivan, Ed, 108
Sunday Express, 185
Sunday Pictorial, 94
Sunday Times, The, 151

Sydney, Sylvia, 80
Sykes, Eric, 90, 91, 92, 96, 101, 117,
  126, 127, 144, 187, 189–90

Take it from here, 96
Tarri, Suzette, 47
Taylor, Elizabeth, 99, 185
Taylor, Robert, 106
Temple, Shirley, 177
Terry-Thomas, 107, 108, 184
Tiller Girls, 86, 92
Tom Jones, 133
Tone, Franchot, 106
Tony Mansell Singers, 168
Tremayne, Mr, 35
Trevallyn, Mr, 123
Trinder, Tommy, 92

Up Pompeii, 188

Variety Band Box, 90
Vaughan, Frankie, 121

Wakefield, Oliver, 43
Walters, Charles, 99, 178
Warrington Opera House, 81–2
Wattis, Richard, 190
Wheeler, Jimmy, 115–16
Whitfield, David, 121
Wilde, Marty, 121
Williams, Cissie, 90
Wilson Keppel and Betty, 43
Winchell, Walter, 100
Withers, Jane, 177
Wonderful Time, 111
Wong, Denis, 135–6
Woods, Harry, 78–9
Wordsworth, William, 51
Worth, Harry, 165